"A beautifully written meditation on the death of a baby and the grief of a family. Wrenching and wry, insightful and outrageously authentic. Andrea Lingle travels where grief takes her, grasping and releasing and ultimately cleaving to the hand of the invisible Holy One whose love reveals itself as so vast only a broken heart could possibly contain it."

— MIRABAI STARR, author of *Caravan of No Despair: A Memoir of Loss & Transformation*

"Andrea Lingle gifts us with a soul-searing honesty about her life, faith, and grief that is rarely exposed to others. If you know the depths of grief, especially the sorrow that accompanies the death of a child, this book holds balm for your heart. It is treasure, born from the darkest of times."

— ALEXANDER JOHN SHAIA, speaker, pilgrim mentor, and author of *Heart and Mind: The Four-Gospel Journey for Radical Transformation*

"This book, in the hands and words of Andrea Lingle, is a mother's testimony written for Gwyneth, her stillborn daughter, and for many who grieve in death's darkness. Through sadness and anger, Lingle writes fiercely to her unanchored self and faith: why did Gwyneth die, why am I still alive? She writes alongside her own children, alongside her friend who shared stillbirth, alongside Jesus and Lazarus and the mothers in Scripture whose children were massacred by King Herod. She writes about encounters in the natural world, the world of her local woods and waters, and the gifts of darkness that awaken space for light in her. With meditations, photos, drawings to shade and color, with poetry, memories, and a newborn faith grammar, Lingle offers a gift to us, too, in our communities and circles, as mothers, sisters, daughters, and members moved by grief, loss, and transforming mercies."

— MELINDA G. FOWL, Licensed Master Social Worker, and Member, North American Association of Christians in Social Work

"*Into a Reluctant Sunrise* touches the heart of a human dilemma: love and loss will always be entwined. Lingle admits that it was not easy to learn to be the parent of a dead child, but feeling Gwyneth still near her, and hearing a small voice ask, 'Can you love me like this?' her reply had to be, 'Yes, I can.'"

— KRISTINE MORRIS, *Foreword Revi*

"Lingle (Credulous), editor of the Missional Wisdom Foundation, mixes poetry, art, and theology to reflect on life and faith after a stillbirth in this gorgeous memoir. After her fourth child dies in the womb, Lingle navigates a long process of aching, angry grief. A Christian, she finds that the comforts of her faith are suddenly meaningless, even offensive, in the face of tragedy. She reevaluates familiar stories like Noah's ark and questions the goodness and existence of God: 'This is a crisis of grammar. Not: Why, God? But: Why God?' Gradually, her faith and identity re-form as she patches together new meaning from ancient sources, particularly the sacraments, and by drawing on the beauty of nature. The book itself becomes part of this patchwork as Lingle creates a space for grieving readers to explore and reconnect to their own spiritual beliefs. As she moves forward, she affirms a faith of doubt and joy mixed with tragedy, and celebrates the ongoing role of her lost daughter in her life: 'If I choose to live in denial of the Divine, I will have to deny the divine within myself and within all my children and my daughter will truly die.' Lingle's intimate, heartfelt story is a soothing balm for the loneliness and disorientation of loss."

—Publishers Weekly

"When Andrea L. Lingle, a Christian mother of three, learned that the baby she carried in her womb had died, her once firm faith in God turned to ashes. *Into a Reluctant Sunrise* is her story of how, despite her devastating grief, she came to embrace the gift of each new day.

"The memoir is moving in revealing how Lingle, a Sunday school teacher and the wife of a minister, learned that faith isn't a guarantee against tragedy. Wounded and brought down by the death of the daughter she'd named Gwyneth, her questions lost their politeness and turned fierce: How could anyone love and serve a God who lets such things happen? Does God care about people's suffering? Does God even exist? With her spiritual practice reduced to 'the equivalent of a newborn's blank, uncomprehending, undemanding stare,' Lingle writes that it was Jesus, and his love for children, who brought her back."

—Kristine Morris, *Foreword* (July / August 2020)

Into a Reluctant Sunrise

MISSIONAL WISDOM LIBRARY
RESOURCES FOR CHRISTIAN COMMUNITY

The Missional Wisdom Foundation experiments with and teaches about alternative forms of Christian community. The definition of what constitutes a Christian community is shifting as many seek spiritual growth outside of the traditional confines of church. Christians are experimenting with forming communities around gardens, recreational activities, coworking spaces, and hundreds of other focal points, connecting with their neighbors while being aware of the presence of God in their midst. The Missional Wisdom Library series includes resources that address these kinds of communities and their cultural, theological, and organizational implications.

Series Editor: Larry Duggins

Into a Reluctant Sunrise

a memoir

Andrea L. Lingle

Illustrations by Casey Arden

Foreword by Luke Lingle

CASCADE *Books* • Eugene, Oregon

INTO A RELUCTANT SUNRISE
A Memoir

Missional Wisdom Library: Resources for Christian Community 9

Cascade Books
An Imprint of Wipf and Stock Publishers
199 W. 8th Ave., Suite 3
Eugene, OR 97401

www.wipfandstock.com

PAPERBACK ISBN: 978-1-5326-6196-9
HARDCOVER ISBN: 978-1-5326-6197-6
EBOOK ISBN: 978-1-5326-6198-3

Cataloguing-in-Publication data:

Names: Lingle, Andrea L., author. | Lingle, Luke, foreword. | Arden, Casey, illustrations.

Title: Into a reluctant sunrise : a memoir / Andrea L. Lingle ; foreword by Luke Lingle ; illustrations by Casey Arden.

Description: Eugene, OR : Cascade Books, 2020 | Missional Wisdom Library: Resources for Christian Community 9

Identifiers: ISBN 978-1-5326-6196-9 (paperback) | ISBN 978-1-5326-6197-6 (hardcover) | ISBN 978-1-5326-6198-3 (ebook)

Subjects: LCSH: Miscarriage—Religious aspects—Christianity. | Bereavement—Religious aspects—Christianity.

Classification: BV4907 .L56 2020 (print) | BV4907 .L56 (ebook)

Manufactured in the U.S.A.   MAY 21, 2020

All line drawings are original artwork by Casey Arden. To see more of her work, see https://www.facebook.com/CaseyArdenArt/.

Thank you to Wendi Bernau for your digital wizardry in bringing the drawings and text together.

To those who mourn . . .

Contents

Acknowledgements

I WOULD LIKE TO thank the following people for giving me the courage I needed to bring this book to print: To Luke Lingle and Chris Osteen for insisting that I can write, and to Dr. Julian for insisting I can't. To Natalie Goldburg for bringing writing practice into the world, and to Christine Hale for bringing it to me. To Larry Duggins and Denise Crane for being willing to read this manuscript with vision. And, most of all, to my family who loves me into trying.

Foreword

EVERY MORNING, LIKE CLOCKWORK, the sun rises. We don't get to decide if it will rise. The sun does not ask for our input, for our thoughts on whether it should rise, or if we are ready for the day. Some days, if the sun were to ask, I think we might tell it to rest a little while longer, maybe stay below the horizon so that we can be wrapped in the inky darkness of night. If pushed, I think there are days that we would rather skip. If the sun didn't rise, would that day, then, be skipped for good?

Into a Reluctant Sunrise is what happens when we embrace a string of sunrises after a sunrise that we never wanted to experience. Andrea leans into the deep grief of a tragic sunrise and demonstrates a path that leads to watching, with expectation, for the sun to rise again.

If there is anything that I have learned in my life of working closely with people, it is that we all have experienced tragedy and grief. In our communities we like to compare and contrast our tragedies; "Oh, that is so much worse," or "I could never do that," but what if there is enough space under the expansive sunrise for all of our grief? What if rather than comparing and contrasting our grief, we all pause and recognize that we all hurt and that we all need to time to heal? Each sunrise offers an opportunity for healing, and it does not matter how many sunrises we need to work out our grief, there is another one coming tomorrow.

Andrea and I experienced an incredible tragedy in our lives, and we still grieve, even as you read this book. And, you know what? That is ok. Grief is not linear or clean. It cannot be put in a box or confined to a certain program or system; however, with each sunrise there is opportunity for healing. With each support group, therapy session, or trip to the gym we take a step on the journey; not a journey to bury our grief but a journey to life that does not ignore the reality of our pain.

If you are reading this and your inner voice begins to tell you that your grief is insignificant or that it is not worthy of the time it takes in your life, then tell that voice to take a break for a little while. Whatever you are hurting from, I am sorry, and I hope you have space to grieve and hope and heal. I hope that even in the midst of a sunrise-not-desired you may feel peace.

Friends, I hope you enjoy this book as much as I did. I hope you allow yourself good space to read this book, be gentle with yourself, color the pages, cry if need be, and know that tomorrow the sun will rise. With each sunrise of the fall and winter of 2013, the spring and summer of 2014, and beyond, Andrea gives us a glimpse of what happens when we embrace the sunrise, even if reluctantly.

Luke Lingle

Introduction

This book is meant to be used. These drawings were designed as meditations. Grief is not something that we talk about, but it is something that we all live with. Casey and I poured our hope and sorrow into the images in this book. They have been designed as coloring meditations. They reflect my journey. I hope they will be a companion on yours.

This is a book about grief.

This is a book about coming of age.

This is a book about
    faith,
        despair,
            hope,

    longing and fear and joy.

This is a memoir of a tiny, silent, still-life.

And it is my story. I left out a few million details. I didn't think it was worth mentioning which treadmill is my favorite at the Y or that I drive a silver mini-van, but I hope the story that you will find here is this: mystery is woven into the fabric of our beings. The answers that used to line the shelves of my mind were worthless to explain the enigma that is grief. Grief isn't a question. I have been knee deep in tears and anger, and the last thing I wanted was an answer. What I wanted was:

space

After something terrible and shattering happens to you, you enter a different world. It's an exclusive club but not a selective one. You become someone who ceases to be just Andrea and becomes Andrea-who-lost-a-child or Derrick-who-had-a-house-fire or Ashley-who-got-cancer. People get really quiet when you walk by. People fumble for words around you. People want to be kind and appropriate and, most of all, somewhere else. Pain is not something people enjoy sitting with.

Tears are unwelcoming.

Impolite.

We are not a culture that grieves well. We are a culture that does things, but when you grieve there is nothing to do: you must be.

You must be for a long, long time.

It takes great courage to engage with the grieving. I could see the panic in the faces of my friends as they entered the realm of grief within which I lived. A kindness and fear casserole.

Questions scrolled across their faces like a stock ticker.

WHAT DO I SAY? WHAT DO I SAY? WHAT DO I SAY? HER? WHAT IF I REMIND HER? WHAT IF I REMIND HER? THE WRONG THING? WHAT IF I SAY THE WRONG THING?

I catch myself thinking that too. "What if this person has just managed to get her terrible tragedy off her mind and I go and bring it up?!?!"

There is never an hour that goes by that I don't think about all my children, so you will hardly be reminding me. Maybe I don't want to cry in front of you, but I haven't forgotten.

Ultimately, most people say the same things. Everyone apologizes. Which is ok, because it seems decent, but unnecessary. What is necessary is to make space for the emotions that accompany grief. If you want to know what to say to a grieving person, here's my overly educated opinion:

Just say . . .

"Tell me your story."

So glad you asked.

Where do I start?

When I began writing this book, I set out to write about the theological voice of nature and I ended up writing a memoir. I didn't want to. Memoir is when people work out their personal demons on paper. Memoir is for people who have climbed a thousand mountains and now sit in leather armchairs sipping Earl Grey and remembering. Memoir is written for the author. Turns out it doesn't matter what I wanted. I wanted to make pretty little piles of words, but my story kept getting in the way. It would catch me in the dark, and I would find myself scribbling away with tears soaking into my collar. It shouldered its way into my writing, and demanded to be heard. So, I wrote it. My memoir. It's a tiny story of a tiny life. It only covers a few months and I didn't go anywhere. Mostly I sat on my steps or my driveway and watched the light change. Because that is what I did for a year after my baby died.

Want some tea?

I have lots

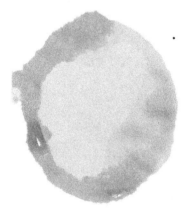

CHAPTER 1

Careless

I LOST A CHILD. No, actually, she died. "Losing a child" is an awkward thing people say because they don't want to say their kid died; is dead. The word dead just sounds so grown up. So humorless. So final. It is the test proctor of words. No smiles, no flexibility, no fun. It stands there all dressed in sensible black, lips pursed and turned down at the corners, not in displeasure, just in unpleasure. The word, death, hasn't smiled even once. So, we, Parents of Dead Children, leave this solemn character alone and prefer to be a society of irresponsible parents.

We had this kid; then we lost her.

Somewhere.

We all do it, because death is hard enough without saying the word, so we settle for losing. Which is also true.

People tell me that they cannot imagine losing a child.

Good. Please, don't imagine it.

It is a terrible thing. It is a thing that consumes your identity and turns your hair grey: I am the mother of a dead child. It has changed me fundamentally. I have become one of the women who cries in public for her very own special reason. I have become a person who knows the comfort of knowing that life is suffering. I have become, but it wasn't easy.

Several years ago, I got my Bachelor's of Science in Nursing. During the course of study, I took an obstetrics class. We learned how to position a mother during labor, how to calculate how many milliliters a golf ball–sized blood clot is, and how to assign an APGAR score. One morning we were taken through the steps of "Caring for The Bereaved Mother." It was all there: how to talk to her therapeutically, which room to put her in (not on the post-partum floor, try gyn-surgery), how to care for her body compassionately, what that mother will need in the years to come that she did not read in *What to Expect*.

Next to the lectern, where the models of the female pelvis or, more memorably, the expanding cervix, usually sat, that day there was a small paper-board box. These boxes are specifically designed to hold the tiny bodies of dead babies. Very sturdy shoe-boxes in which to wrap up nine months of dreams like a dead kitten. We passed one of these boxes around the classroom—reluctantly. This was something no one wanted to hold hands with.

- Cabbage leaves on breast → dry up milk
- Heat will ease pain
- Do not express milk
- Pain ↓ 3-5 days
- If red streaks → call provider

There are a lot of unfortunate things you work with as a nurse that are secretly thrilling—tubes and chemicals so powerful that they can alter the course of life and death. With a few drops of liquid, I could obliterate the pain of having thirty-seven staples in your stomach. With some other drops, I could change the pressure of your blood. With a tube and a large needle I could drip someone else's blood into your body without killing you. I once told someone I became a nurse because I love pushing buttons. And there are so many buttons, so many fantastic buttons.

But that little box was sobering, a tiny reminder that chemicals and buttons don't even begin to brush the truth of caring for people who are hurting. I don't remember holding it. I must have because we all did, but I don't remember it.

But I remember mine. Thick white paper with yellow seeds and flowers mixed into it.

We were told to encourage the parents to hold their dead baby and to clip a lock of his or her hair. We were instructed to dress and clean the baby. I took careful notes on how to educate the mother about dealing with the pain of engorgement when birth did not deliver life that needs nourishment.

I found out later that there are matching boxes for all the tiny bits of the baby's minute life. All the little tags and footprint cards that might be in a baby book, but probably won't, especially now. My box ties shut with yellow ribbon. Our baby did not have enough hair to clip. My nurses took pictures and footprints. Cabbage leaves do not dry up milk fast enough.

When our baby was delivered, there was a brief moment that she was lying on the foot of the bed looking perfect. She wasn't blue or broken. She was beautiful. She looked exhausted. She had tried so hard to live, but she hadn't. My husband, Luke, and I looked at her wanting her to scream and breathe and simply be not dead. Anything but dead. Luke gathered her up tenderly. So gentle and broken. He is a big man, and she looked tiny and precious in his arms. She was warm when I held her, but it was my heat. The warmth of my womb that had been powerless to protect her. Somehow, that was the worst part. She felt warm. She felt asleep. Tiny joints and lips, beautiful and perfect, but lost beyond the world I was forced to inhabit. I held her, searching her face for a twitch or a breath, some sign that this was a Disney movie and all we had to do was chafe her little back and all would be well.

Years ago, when my third child was barely crawling, I took my kids to a friend's house for lunch. My first three kids are thirty-seven months apart. With a three-year-old, a one-and-a-half-year-old, and an infant, you don't get many lunch invitations, but this friend is terribly brave. I love to chat, and one of the hardest parts of being a stay-at-home parent is that you don't get much opportunity for chat. Every word you manage to say is usually related to organizing small, distractible persons. Or finding shoes. *Finding Shoes*, could be the title of an era of my life.

"Do you remember when we had that blue wading pool?"

"Oh yes, that was during the *Finding Shoes* era."

What is it like to be the parent of several simultaneously small children? It is exactly like trying to herd shoes.

But Miss Judy didn't care if my kids arrived with shoes on or not or asked questions or not or touched the things on her shelves or her face. Miss Judy sat on the floor and touched the things on her shelves with them.

Miss Judy collects nativity sets and displays them year-round. Each shelf is like a tiny booth in a Middle-Eastern market, beckoning each child to come and play. It is always almost Christmas at Miss Judy's house.

After we ate lunch—cold cuts complete with tiny sweet pickles in a dish—the kids played with the nativity sets and she told me her story of the birth of her second baby, a stillborn. As I listened to the words fall like dust motes onto the carpet all around us, there was a tiny part of me, the eternal part that is made of stardust and God, the part for which time isn't, that began to tremble. I was not yet pregnant with the baby I lost and it had been twenty years past for her, but something in me knew that we shared this thing.

Her story intersected mine in the place of spirit that dwells outside of chronology, and questions tumbled out of me.

"Did you have to go through labor?"

"Yes."

"I can't imagine having to go through labor knowing that the baby was dead."

"Yeah. It was terrible."

She was holding a blanket in her hands twisting it slowly. Not in anguish. It was as if she was just slowly wringing out two decades of time and tears. I drew designs in the carpet with my finger and absently handed Oliver, my third child, a baby at the time, a four-inch, stuffed Jesus to chew on. It was an important space we were in, but it was not a comfortable one.

"Did your milk come in?"

"Yes."

"Oh."

Sympathetic resonation is a phenomenon that is, over-simply, when two things are enough alike that vibration in one triggers vibration in the other.

Some pain seems unfair.

    Miss Judy came to my baby's funeral. There were tears in her eyes. They were only partially for me.

We resonate sympathetically, she and I.
Me and she.
We.

"Together"

I am here.
And somewhere inside
A voice echoed
Or answered
    So am I.
And arm and arm we went,

Together.

Blue Sky

WHEN YOU GO INTO the hospital as a pregnant lady, they send you to labor and delivery triage. No one else in a hospital wants a pregnant lady. If you need to go to the emergency room for, say, a broken leg, you should consider first being eight or nine months pregnant. Fast track. You won't even get to sit down in the waiting room. They shove you in a wheel chair and speed-walk you to the labor and delivery floor. My guess is that if you walk in as a visitor, if you are pregnant enough, you will probably be accosted by terrified persons with wheel chairs.

Triage is the last test before you can truly become a parent. When a pregnant woman reaches the last bit of pregnancy, the only thing on her mind (and, incidentally, anyone else's related to her), waking or sleeping, is, "Am I in labor?" You are told you will be able to tell the difference between the extreme discomfort of being horribly pregnant and the extreme discomfort of labor, but, as the relativity of time becomes real, you stare
each
stupid
minute

in the face, forcing yourself to walk and hope and analyze every twitch of your miserable body. The two things you fear the most are being in labor and not knowing and not being in labor and not knowing. So, you time contractions you think are painful hoping to find a pattern and you call your friend and ask "Do you think this sounds right?" and your partner tries not to ask if you have felt any "real contractions" and your mom tries not to call again, and finally, you get twelve precious contractions in one hour and you go.

To Labor and Delivery Triage.

So far, you have been managing. You have been breathing and you got in the shower and, now, you are here, and they want you to sit on a table that is always just a bit too high for your encumbered body to slide onto. They want you to sit still, but it is starting to hurt in earnest, but they have to make sure you are really in labor.

Are you sure?
Are you ready?
Are you in labor?

If you are far enough along with real labor you get to proceed to A Room, if you aren't, they send you home. To wait. Some more.

When I arrived in Labor and Delivery triage for the first time, I had already been laboring at home for twenty-four hours. One entire day. I hadn't slept. It hurt. I was dilated to two.

The standard triage procedure is to change into a hospital gown while the nursing staff strap two, round monitors (that look like the things you get at restaurants to let you know your table is ready) to your giant, petulant stomach. Then you sit for twenty minutes while they monitor the baby's heartbeat and measure any contractions you may be having. They do a cervical check to see if those contractions have been productive. "Just a few more minutes, honey. Just try to sit still so the monitor can get a good reading." All while your body is fiercely trying to force a person out through the straight and narrow.

When I was in labor with my second child, I arrived at the hospital well past the affable stage. My husband stopped the car in the valet parking line and I simply got out and started walking. I was stopped every two or three minutes by Purposeful and Productive contractions. When the wheelchair orderly scooped me up, I did not talk to him. I was not polite. I did not care what his name was or that he was a divine creation. That was the only time I got to skip triage. I guess I looked like a person who might just have a baby where I stood.

Triage is a nervous place. If you are in labor, it is a painful place. If you aren't, it's painful too. The light seems yellow and green and brown and the sheets are worn thin and stiff with washing and pressing. And you sit and wait for the news. Where will you go? Will you go home with balloons and a bundle of warm, squidgy baby or a tiny paperboard box full of a few pictures, a tag, a footprint, and the echo of the kicks that never came.

A still life wrapped in my flesh.

A shy death all silent and dark.

The sky was crisply blue. An October sky. It was warm and brilliant. It was a day that had gathered together and breathed gently into my life. My children giggled and chased each other around the church playground; alone and together. Just us. I was thirty-eight weeks pregnant. It had been a very difficult pregnancy. At thirteen weeks, I remember lying on the floor of the bathroom while my older kids took a bath, too weak and nauseated to raise my head. By the third trimester I was reduced to sitting in a red plastic Adirondack chair that had been run over a few times, folding laundry while my kids swung on the A-frame metal swing set in our back yard.

Earlier that year my first child, Laine, started kindergarten at home. We had counted and colored and ABC'd our way through September, but by October, I was looking for ways to keep my kids safe without having to move. I was desperately tired. Frighteningly tired. They said it was because I had had so many children so quickly, but the why wasn't helping. After breakfast, I would camp out in Laine's bed, reclining on my left side, counting kicks and playing songs for them to dance to. "Again, Mommy, again." There were so many tears. My mother called a friend to clean my house. There was concern behind people's voices. It was a difficult pregnancy.

That October day I had decided to bring the kids to the playground at the church where my husband served as a pastor because it was fenced in and no one was likely to be there. I wouldn't have to chase them or worry about them offending anyone. We could see Daddy's office window from the playground and he would come to the window and wave and we would shout and wave back. I sat on the bench with my swollen feet propped in a chair and chatted to my mother on the phone. She mentioned that I sounded more cheerful. I was. It was a gentle moment. There wasn't much bickering. Across Church Street, the Episcopalian church's bell quartered the hours. The minutes of my life neatly tallied and corded; stacked in the corner. It was a peaceful, ordinary day.

Only the baby hadn't kicked. I sat; waiting. She lay; quiet. Her soul hovering for one last day of peace. One last gentle day of laughter and blue sky.

Such a beautiful blue sky.

Eventually we must have decided to go home. I don't remember that part. We have gathered ourselves up so many times to leave that church that that time doesn't stand out. I don't remember the rest of that afternoon either. It's odd what you do remember when the mundane becomes indelible. I was blanching broccoli to freeze when the neatly stacked minutes tipped over and I couldn't wait one more for the baby to kick. I just walked out of the kitchen and went to my bedroom, lay down on my left side and waited. You are supposed to feel ten kicks in an hour during periods of a baby's wakefulness, but I hadn't felt one all day. I poked her and laid an ice pack on my belly to wake her up while tears soaked my sheets. We decided to go to the hospital. The broccoli was spread out all over the kitchen on pans ready to be frozen, and I just left it there. A tiny clear-cut forest; vibrantly green. Someone finished packing it into jars, but I could never bring myself to eat it. After a year-and-a-half, I finally threw it away.

This time in triage I wasn't in pain. There were no contractions. I sat cross-legged in a room I remember to be all blue and green. The bed was terribly uncomfortable. It seemed more machine than furniture. I sat and stared at the bed sheets letting words that meant nothing fall out of my mouth. Luke said some words back. The words cemented together and created a patchwork dam that held back a veritable river of disaster.

They belted the monitor paddles on my stretched and scarred belly with reserved, therapeutic smiles. There was only one heartbeat—mine. The midwife squirted more of the clear ultrasound gel onto the paddle in hopes that a better signal would be all that was needed to resurrect a broken heart. My whole belly was covered in cold ultrasound jelly when I rolled into the arms of my husband and we wept the first of a thousand tears.

I am so glad I had that day with her. It was beautiful. When the ultrasound confirmed that she was gone, lost, dead, and I found my hours scattered and ruined, I remembered those minutes wrapped in bell-song, tidily stowed away in memory, as the last hours we had—before.

CHAPTER 3

Expert

WHEN I GOT HOME, after the family left and the dinners stopped coming, I began the long process of becoming one with a tragic past. There were other children to feed and dress and raise. There was a life left to spend one way or another. There were stages of grief to navigate.

Grief is a sneaky bastard. Apparently, he waits, lounging in the corner, eyes half-closed, waiting for the perfect time to hurtle in and choke his victim not-quite-to death. Sometimes Grief catches you minding your own business, just doing some laundry or sweeping the kitchen floor and then you are sitting in a pile, laundry or dust, blowing snot bubbles.

But there are the times you can see him there. Waiting. You know he's coming and you can feel your butt hole running for your belly button. Or that's how I feel when I tense up for the blow I know is coming. During that first winter, most afternoons at one o'clock, I would haul my twenty-seven pound two-year-old son, Oliver, up the stairs for his nap.

One, two buckle my . . . SHOE! Three, four shut the . . . DOOR!

After, I changed his diaper, and laid him down in his bed, grief would attack me at the top of the stairs.

Ollie, ballie, Ollie, ballie bee, sittin' on your mama's knee,

The corners of my vision contracted
to a single, unnavigable image: all those steps.
All those brown, carpeted steps.
Those steps that wouldn't be needing a baby gate after all.
I would sit down
     on the second or third step,
waiting for enough breath
       to continue—choked by the huge isn't

There isn't a crib where there was going to be a crib.
There isn't a song where there was going to be a song.
There isn't a voice where there was going to be a voice.

Life ceased before breath began. Still-born. Still life. Still death. Still sitting on the stairs staring out the window at the tangled branches and power lines. Waiting for enough breath to continue; the breath that never came for her, but does come, at last, for me.

Sitting on the stairs.

Between places.

Waiting.

I am not too far into my life as a grieving parent, but I have my ten thousand hours. Malcolm Gladwell wrote a book called, *Tipping Point*, in which he writes that to become an expert in an area a person must spend ten thousand hours in practice. That's a little over four hundred sixteen days without sleeping. But that's what they give you the sleeping pills for.

Elisabeth Kübler-Ross and David Kessler wrote the book on grieving. They describe the Five Stages of Grief: denial, anger, bargaining, depression, and acceptance. I visited them all. I have gone through them in order, backwards, sidewise, and in looping aerobatics. I learned that there are Things To Do when you are faced with Situational Depression. I exercised vigorously, I chewed off the edges of sleeping pills, I drank scotch on Thursdays, I texted friends, I threw stuff, I Engaged Purposefully with my children, I manically cleaned my kitchen sink. I did all of that. On loop.

Grieving, it turns out, is similar to gratitude. Both are feelings that become a lifestyle. Both focus on something important in your life. Both can change you forever. Only one will leave you sobbing on a Tuesday afternoon, unable to make lunch for your kids, limed by anger so profound that mosquitoes will explode into tiny fire clouds after biting you. I made up that last bit.

"Mama, I'm hungry." My children stood in the kitchen, waiting for lunch. *Three faces, three mouths, three voices, six eyes, six pieces of bread, peanut butter, what about carrots, peel six carrots, no three carrots, and fruit, you can't feed them like this, what parent feeds their kids like this,*

"Alright, honey,"

honey for the sandwiches, three plates, cups, water with ice and a straw, milk, milk,

"I can't do this."

And I was standing in the garage slowly banging my head on the window of the mini-van that had one empty seat.

"Mama, I made lunch. Please, Mama, come inside. I know you're sad. I made lunch. I couldn't peel the carrots, so I just washed them. Come on, Mama."

"Ok, baby. I'm so sorry. I'm so sorry. I just couldn't do it." Those tears burned down my face. He was six. They ate their lunch. They told me jokes. I actually laughed. My head was bruised for days.

Of all the stages of grief, anger is the most difficult for me. Anger is hard to get rid of and it's hard to control. You can pound it out on a treadmill or talk it out in a "safe space," but, most of the time, it just quietly builds up until it hisses out like steam from a teakettle. It is emotional nonsense, and it hurts everyone around you. There are moments when you are mid-shriek, shaking with rage, and you realize—you have no idea what you're screaming about. And that just makes you more angry. Biting, scratching, hitting angry. The light from the bedside table backlit my blotchy, tear-blurred face. I spattered invectives at Luke's face. I have no idea what we had been fighting about. I didn't know then. I just knew I was angry. Really, really, terribly angry. I felt the rage coil up like power inside me, and I hit him with a leather boot. His side was bruised for days.

I hate that part of this story.

I am a lily of the valley: small, pale, and tender. When I was a teenager I lived at least fifty percent of my life in Victorian novels. I poured my heart out into my journals in painfully stilted prose. I sketched dresses with empire waistlines then made them out of muslin and wore them to church. There weren't many thorns in the garden of my life, and, if there was any anger, it wasn't allowed to speak. It was the penniless cousin in the corner embroidering the napkins.

Anger has been solidly incorporated into my life now. I am harder, drawn-in, resentful, unwilling to believe that today could possibly bring joy.

I never know what I am going to get. Some days I wake up and the sun has painted the world in color and light and I am chock full of personhood, but other days the cavern of my mind is darkened by brown, swirling clouds that nothing but the most determined effort can dispel. I am basically a noxious tincture of sadness and anger. On those angry days, terrible words bounce around in my head. Cord accident. Low-birth weight. Caffeine. Listeria.

Listeria is a bacterium you can ingest in lunchmeats or sushi. If you are infected, most of the time, you don't even feel sick, but it can cause late-term fetal death. Three people have asked me if I thought it was listeria that killed by baby. They didn't mean it. They couldn't help it. They didn't think. I could see their minds beginning to whir, excited by a mystery. Their gazes turned inward as their minds flipped through the possible causes of a full-term baby dying without warning.

A mystery, once solved, makes tragedy less random.
If you can avoid these things, then it won't happen to you.

I know an answer would be nice, but I just don't think I could handle knowing it was an illicit ham sandwich that killed my baby.

Anger loves blame. They sit and make out in the back seat of your mind. I tried blame on anyone within arm's length. I held up swatches to see who wore it best. I blamed the health-care providers. I blamed the baby. I blamed God. I blamed myself. Even as I dressed each guest in the macabre vestments, I knew it was all pretend. Grief and Anger were just playing dress up in the worst way. I knew that my baby's death was something that happened. I knew it was no one's fault, but when does knowing something, *believing* something, help when you are so angry it leaves bruises?

Anger hates being placated. It does not want to hear your reasonable thoughts. It does not want to know it will all be ok. It wants things to be terrible—just for a moment. Let me have my tears. Let me have my anguish. Let me have my despair. Just for a moment.

When Christmas rolled around I hid in my closet, weeping, because God didn't let God's son die and my baby did. I know. I do realize that God's son did die, but not until Good Friday. They had so long together before he died. Like eternity. And, honestly, that is how I felt. I couldn't talk myself into rationality or reasonability.

I did not want to hear songs about a perfect child born on a perfect night. My child was perfect and no crying did she make, but when I held her, for those blurred minutes or hours, I had to fight down a scream of horror as I watched her lips turn black and her blistered skin begin to sag. There would be no crib for her head, only tears and ashes.

Anger made me real.

For the first time, I didn't care about the right answers. The veneer of righteousness peeled away, leaving a soul willing to bleed all over the floor and unable to keep it together for anyone's sake. I took the entire library of my faith, knowledge, and wisdom, and tore out every single page. All those carefully curated systems of belief that I had dragged behind me for thirty-two years that had informed every decision, been my bedfellow, and given me such a straight path to walk, sat, torn and scattered, unable to comfort or confront. Systematic theology, systematically destroyed. I could think and be exactly who I was because it didn't matter anymore. There was no one left to please. Answers hadn't saved her or me.

On my second birthday, my parents moved from the peaks of the Rocky Mountains to the tidewater of coastal Virginia before settling, four years later, in central North Carolina. My mother, raised Catholic but out of practice, wanted to raise her children in church. My father's only religious past had been in Lutheran South Dakota. They began attending the Methodist church. Its main qualification for becoming my crucible of faith and doctrine was that it was within walking distance of our two-story brick house and didn't offend anyone.

Thus began my illustrious career as a person called Methodist. I encountered the God of Abraham, Moses, and Aaron. I found the American Jesus and wondered daily what he would do. I read the Bible, went to Sunday school more or less on time, and covered the margins of my bulletin with notes. I cared deeply about having the right answers and I knew them all. Even the tough ones.

I could find Nahum without using the index, I had the word of God hidden in my heart, I could recite the prayers and creeds. Humorous side note: when my mother, dutiful Catholic and homeschool mom, was teaching me the Apostles' Creed, there was a transcendent moment when, proudly reciting from memory, I cleared up one of the mysteries of our faith in one misbegotten sentence: "*I believe in Jesus Christ, his only son, Our Lord, who was conceived by Pontius Pilot . . .*" My mother stared at me, horrified by the realization that she would have to stone her first child.

For me, faith was a matter of acing the test. All you needed to do was study hard and get a good night's sleep and Blam-oh! Life well lived! I have always secretly loved taking tests. I am sure that good athletes have a similar reaction to sporting events. I wouldn't know because when faced with a physical challenge I just want to throw up, but give me a Scantron sheet and a No. 2 pencil, and I am a warrior.

I took the SAT when 1600 was a perfect score. The day I took it, we were all sorted into navy blue plastic chairs in an English classroom at the local high school. Our No. 2 pencils, calculators, and little slips of paper with our scribbled social security numbers sat arranged on the desks. I was like a racehorse walking to the starting gate. I was sweating pure joy. This test was written for me (actually, I am a white American, so it *was* written for me).

In the middle of the test, probably about the second or third math section, my future was shaping up nicely. I had hit a few rough patches, but I was pretty sure I had figured out enough to land me safely in the middle class. Suddenly, I noticed that the soft-edged boy sitting next to me was getting up to leave. He just took his test, his answer sheet, and his No. 2 pencil and walked out.

He left a puddle on his seat.

Grief will do that to you. You sit in a pungent puddle knowing that the answers, whatever they are, don't matter. Not anymore.

Answers. Answers were so important to me. God was this way, and did this, and if you do that, this will happen. Say the words, have your quiet time, be good, don't touch, don't swear. I could wrap myself up in my answers and be safe. I knew where I was, who I was, and where I was going. My God was a deity spun of answers. And, like cotton candy in the rain, my God melted. In an anger born of betrayal, I hauled out all my answers and dumped them on the table.

Everything out in the open where I could see it.

Right and wrong.

Black and white.

Cause and effect.

Now, there are no more answers. There is just being alive for me, and not being alive for her. What seems anachronistic is, while it feels like my life is turning brown and crumbling, like one of last year's autumn leaves, I have never been so present and immediate. Sitting on Miss Judy's floor listening to her story of Stillbirth, I imagined what it must have been like for her. I thought her whole life would stop. I figured the train engine would sit, immobile, until its wheels rusted tight to the rails while all of life chugged past. But it isn't like that. Most of the time, time seems to expand. Everything is drawn in prismacolor.

I had no more answers to predict the future or explain the past, so I mostly lived entirely in the moment. One moment stacked end to end with another. Photons of life. Discrete packets. Me with my ruined answers piled all around me, blown directly out of the hypothetical. All the words that had formed all my answers got tangled up and began looking like the remains of a burned-out iron works piled up on a hollow altar. Grotesque angles and curves that once held meaning but were now sooty tangles unable to articulate the faith of an intellectual.

We baptized her Gwyneth Elise Lingle in the hospital. Pastor Rob brought a silver communion cup as a font. She wore my mother's baptismal gown. She didn't cry.

I did.

When Luke baptized Laine, Luke wore a cross made of metal nails on a leather cord. When he baptized Annabel, our second, he wore a beautiful filigree cross. Oliver's cross is bright silver. Their crosses will be given to them at their confirmations should they choose to be confirmed. Gwyneth's little wooden cross was cremated with her a few days after her baptism.

We had a funeral for her. There was a knitted frog and a stuffed bear on the pulpit. The organist played *Twinkle, Twinkle Little Star*. I cried out loud while Annabel danced in the aisle in a pink princess costume. I stared at the tear-blurred colors of the stained-glass window while my womb bled and the untapped milk in my breasts ached and I leaned on my husband as if he wasn't dissolving too.

I shook hands and received hugs and watched dimly as other people cared for my children. Meals and activities were delivered. We called the hospital to get her death certificate. We went to the funeral home to collect her ashen remains. And I became one of the hollow-eyed, careless parents who lost a child. One for whom there are support groups. One for whom stairs are metaphorical and laughter and sunshine are prescribed therapy.

CHAPTER 4

The Valley

"Do you want to hold her?"

The first time I held a new baby after mine died, I was sitting in the back pew at church with a woman I knew who had a six-week-old baby girl. Mine would have been eight weeks old. She met my eyes, not like the acquaintances we were, but directly, woman to woman, mother to mother, completely aware of all the implications of her question.

"Do you want to hold her?"

Until that moment, I had only thought about it in the hypothetical.

What would I do?
Cry?
Get angry?
Run?
Run with the baby?

I dreamed about babies being dropped off on my doorstep or handed to me in parking lots. I had thought about advertising to be a wet nurse. I had thought about adopting a teenage mother so I could help her raise her child. Hormones, friends. The struggle is real.

"Yes." I didn't bother with polite gushing. I gathered her up with the confidence of a mother who has held babies in the darkest hours of the night, comforting them with the power of her body while the world slept.

"She is beautiful."

She was a beautiful baby. She was small with tiny brown hairs on her forehead that flowed with an invisible stream down the bridge of her nose. Her lips were pressed together with a firmness that made me smile ruefully. She would not be tossed about by the whims of others. She would be fiery.

"She doesn't look anything like my babies."

I saw her relax. I wasn't going to run. This little bundle of reflexes and fuzzy hair wasn't mine, and no other baby would be. I would never hold my baby again.

After that the dreams stopped.

But Christmas didn't. Christmas came, and this time it was more personal. More poignant. God's son wasn't still-born because the world needed him. The world needed to see Jesus grow up and be a man and say things and heal people and give sermons, so he was born.

The world needed Gwyneth too.

I grew up singing in a children's choir. The director, John, taught me many things, but one of the things that formed me was his love of and respect for text.

It may have actually changed my life when he stood in front of us and read Robert Frost's poem, "Stopping by Woods on a Snowy Evening." I remember he read the opening line, "Whose woods these are, I think I know," and stopped and looked at us.

Then he read it again.

And again.

That third time, sixty third-through-ninth-grade kids stopped wiggling and listened. And heard. And saw.

> Whose woods these are, I think I know.
> His house is in the village though;
> He will not see me stopping here
> To watch his woods fill up with snow.

I still see the same image in my mind when I hear those words.

Sometimes when your life changes, you know. You get married or get divorced, choose a career or lose one, give birth to or bury your daughter; but, sometimes, you don't know. Sometimes you just look back on an afternoon and see your knobby knees and thick bangs and know that that afternoon changed you forever.

Mostly those moments when he stopped the music and read aloud to us were beautiful, but there was one text he brought to us that broke my heart forever. I was sitting on the back row, about eight seats in, when he told us the story of Herod's massacre of the innocents, and we read the text of The Coventry Carol together— line by line.

The Coventry Carol is a song of lament both gentle and grotesque. The tune, The French Carol, is sad but soothing. Exactly what you would sing to your fretful child who was too tired to sleep. A child you knew would be dead in the morning. A child whom you could not save.

This story hit me like a train.

Herod said what? And the soldiers obeyed him?

There are just some moments in this long, broad swath of history that stand out like oil rigs in a bird sanctuary. Things so ludicrously terrible that there seems to be no way to explain them. If humans are indeed created beings endowed with the image of the Creator, how can you explain a man willing to murder babies to preserve his political power. Three camel riding dudes coming to worship a child scared him so much he ordered his great big adult soldiers to march out and kill babies. That right there is psychological guano.

Bat shit crazy.

> *Lullay, Thou little tiny Child,*
> *By, by, lully, lullay.*
> *Lullay, Thou little tiny Child.*
> *By, by, lully, lullay.*

The Massacre of the Innocents is not part of the Christmas story that we tell our children around the tree on Christmas morning, and it has never been a part of any Christmas pageant I have ever seen. It is terrible.

I imagine there were not very many women living within sword point of Herod who put Mary on their Christmas card list. My guess is that they weren't all that fascinated with the gifts the magi had brought. I am pretty sure they felt like the express to Egypt should have been standing room only. How could God leave our children to die while Jesus fled to Egypt? Where was my dream-warning? Was my baby too insignificant to save?

Was *my* baby too insignificant to save?

I love to think that the story of Advent is all about the coming of a great teacher of love and inclusivity and social justice, and it seems to be except for the part where some guy KILLS ALL THE BABIES!

> O sisters, too, how may we do,
> For to preserve this day;
> This poor Youngling for whom we sing,
> By, by, lully, lullay.

I hate this story. It is all the worst of life rolled into one little, tiny excerpt. I want to yell and scream and protest that this is not the God that saves the adulteress from stoning or notices Zacchaeus in the tree. This is an Olympian God who promotes God's agenda and if all the babies die . . . well, the hero escapes, so it's ok.

I hear the voice of the Psalmist raging out, "How long, O Lord? Will you forget me forever?"

WHY WAS MINE NOT SAVED?

Herod the King, in his raging,
Charged he hath this day;
His men of might, in his own sight,
All children young, to slay.

Now I, along with the sisters, too, understand how it feels to know that the sunrise will find me with a dead baby in my arms, feeling the weight of all those dark hours, and not knowing if I will ever be able move forward. How will I ever make sense of my "nights of weeping, my days of lament?[1]"

This story, and many like it, aren't told under the twinkling lights. In fact, our choir never performed the Coventry Carol that year. I don't know why we didn't; perhaps it was unutterably sad.

Unutterable, actually.

Probably we didn't learn it fast enough for the Christmas concert and it had to be cut for practicality, but I always thought it must have been too sad to sing publically. It was a song to be learned and absorbed, but not sung. Not out loud.

Maybe it would have been too horrible for sixty kids to stand up and sing about wholesale murder with perfectly blended voices, but then again, it might not have been. It might have been a beautiful space for grief.

I have discovered that there is no griefatorium in our society. There are moments when I feel the grief roll in, like a wave off the ocean, and the tears start rolling down my face and my lungs start jumping. I am sure it isn't a classy cry. There is usually snot involved. When I find a small corner to sit and unpack all these questions and beat my fists against the walls, I scramble to tidy it all away if I am discovered. I don't want to be discovered.

Awkward.
Embarrassing.
Not Cool.

Our society is so uncomfortable with the wretched things in life it often refuses to even let them be wretched. Platitudes fly into the space of grief at a pace just faster than thought. Who cares if it's true or not? Take it from a member of the club; it hurts.

But these platitudes keep difficult things off our own doorsteps. If that thing that happened to them is God's plan, then it must mean that it was purposeful. Not random. Not going to happen to me. If good will come of it, and good might, then, *in the long run*, it is ok. Not meaningless. If you can bear it, it will make you stronger.

"All things work together for good,"
"God has a plan,"
"God will never give you more than you can bear,"

These words take something painful and place it firmly in the category of painful-but-therapeutic. Like the death of my baby is the emotional equivalent of push-ups. Please. Not yet. I need terrible things to be terrible for just a little while. Losing my baby is really, really awful, and I don't need anyone to rush me through to healing. Not just yet.

Not helpful.
Not kind.
Not what I want to hear right now.

Those children died at Herod's hand and hell came to earth and, although we all know now that Jesus would come bringing a new movement to the souls of men and women, he could have come just as powerfully without all the baby-blood. And God can do good things in my life without baby-ashes.

Then woe is me, poor Child, for Thee,
And ever mourn and say;
For Thy parting, nor say nor sing,
By, by, lully, lullay.

I don't want to be joyful. I don't want to celebrate the joy of someone else's baby swaddled and smelling of pure love. I don't want to sit on the floor in the back of my darkened closet, beating on my dry breasts and raging at the God who did not save, the God who did not save the children left behind when Joseph fled to Egypt, the God who let the baby in my womb drift beyond my grasp.

Quiet
Corners of
Choking grief turn
Into expanses
Of infinite
Silence

CHAPTER 5

Chaos

THE PROBLEM WITH GRIEF is that it messes with your equilibrium. The balance between faith and doubt tips disturbingly. Questions lose their soft politeness and turn fierce.

It seems cliché and predictable, but I am five-stages-of-grief-angry. I don't want to be angry because it means I am on a well-worn trail of tears. Oh, here's the angry phase. I had put my trust in God and God failed. I am like a tragic circus act.

Watch me while I now blame God for this grief I am feeling!!!

But the problem is, I don't blame God.

Not anymore.

For so long I have toiled down this path of faith,
but I have stopped walking,
my feet stuck in the
tear-salty mud,
and I am
refusing
to take
another
step.

I will not follow this way unintentionally.
This is a crisis of grammar.

Not: Why, God?   But: Why God?

Why God...

CHAOS

....Is God?

Who wants to love and serve a God who is either too callous or careless to keep your children safe—even when you ask nicely? Who wants to believe in such a God? Surely, chaos is better than that.

Isn't that the alternative to Purpose?

The world is a chaotic system built by chance and the drive to disseminate genetic material in the most beneficial way for each species. Those that die without passing on their genetic code become irrelevant in this system. They are gratuitous uses of resources.

Even through the haze of grief I realize that I am being somewhat melodramatic. Can thirty-two years of faith crumble under the weight of a five-pound, twelve-ounce death? Prior to our vaccinated, fluoridated, sanitized life, many parents lived to bury their children. I know that. But still, there is the story of Noah.

I married a preacher. I teach Sunday School. I hate the story of Noah.

Recap:

God thinks the world is terrible.

God is fed up with humans and decides to undo them. God tells one guy who seems to be a decent chap to build a huge boat and take two of every animal, male and female, no wait, maybe seven of the birds, we will be needing them to make our holy sacrifices, and get those animals into the arky, arky. Then it rains for forty days and the whole world floods and everyone dies except Noah, his family, and his animals. Then God promises via rainbow to never. do. that. again.

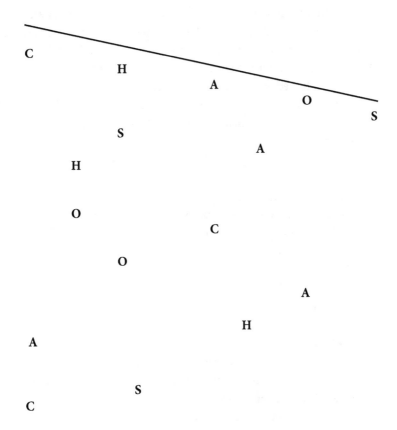

Sunday Schools love this story. It is in all the Children's Bibles. We plaster our church nurseries with this story. When Oliver was born, we bought Annabel a toy Noah set to give her as we left for the hospital. It was supposed to keep her entertained while we were gone. It was adorable. There were chubby little animals all cozily paired up, and a gnomish Noah with an olive branch bearing bird on his hand. Even the elephants were grinning. She was eighteen months old. She loved the animals. I thought it was nice. But somewhere under the plastic preciousness there was a sinister message: go to bed at night or we will undo you.

I have been handed dozens of Sunday School guides for teaching this story. One included making tiny arks out of graham crackers and chocolate pudding. I didn't take them up on that one.

I try to avoid situations where I am responsible for a dozen preschoolers in their Sunday-best sealing graham cracker arks with chocolate pudding.

"Ok boys and girls. Let's put the sides on our arks. Now what did God tell Moses to put on the ark?"

"The animals!"

"Who else?"

"His family!"

"Anyone else?"

"NO!"

"Why?"

"Because everyone else was bad and needed to die!"

"Very good children! Now, what do we learn from this story?"

"God loves us very much."

There is a logical fallacy there somewhere. I never took logic, so I am very insecure about committing fallacies or spotting them, but even I can smell that one. How is the "take home point" that God loves you or God promises to save you or anything besides don't screw up or God will fry you like an ant under a magnifying glass? It just doesn't make sense. If there is a message in this story it is that God is probably going to exterminate humankind out of sheer frustration—just not by flood.

God promised.

This story has survived, first from teller to teller, then from writer to reader from the beginnings of the human story. It is mythic and huge, and reveals something very important about humans from way back. Humans want to know why. The story of Noah asks the same question you and I are trying to ask every single day.

Why does really bad stuff happen?

Really bad stuff. Floods, hurricanes, earthquakes, children dying, and, *if* God is out there, how could *this* have happened? Surely a good God wouldn't have let *that* happen unless there was a reason.

Because everyone must, sooner or later, face the perpetual, cliché question. If God is and God is good, why does bad stuff happen? Not just to me, but at all. Not the everyday pain of life or the avoidable pain that comes from making bad decisions, the big, unjust, how-do-I-explain-this-to-my-kids kinds of pain. Can't God just come down or up or over and fix the really bad, unproductive pain?

There are millions of stories about how people, pressed through pain, find strength and wisdom along the way, and, yes, that is good, but isn't that an outcome and not a purpose? And it doesn't always work together for good, and even if it did, isn't that a heavy-handed way to run a system. Couldn't an all-powerful being accomplish good without near total annihilation?

The writers and tellers of the flood story believed that the flood was a punishment from God. Perhaps they needed to find a way to assure themselves that a flood like that wouldn't happen again tomorrow or the next day if they were very, very good . . . throw in a sacrifice or two, just to be safe.

What if, instead of a story of punishment, the flood account was a story told to try to explain a natural, albeit apocalyptic, event?

That one is almost harder than the angry God theory. I am not equipped to face a God who does not intervene in the face of overwhelming, impending disaster. Apparently, the whole world drowned. Were prayers going directly to voicemail? Perhaps God is a careless parent. Perhaps God tells God's friends that God lost a few million children.

Perhaps God isn't.

(Not, not a careless parent. Just not.)

Life seems too chaotic, too random, to support religion. I look around and can't find evidence of a loving God in the tableaux of endemic poverty, brutal addiction, and religious intolerance. Divine promises have been revealed as light refracted through the curved lens of a water droplet. Religion as an institution is no longer necessary. The smart phone is now Marx's opiate for the masses. Faith is for the superstitious.

What we know is the speed of light. $3.00 \times 10^8 \, m/s$

What we know is the mass of hydrogen. $1.67 \times 10^{-24} \, g$

What we know is that these mountains are old. $\sim 400 \, million \, years$

But there is no evidence of God. Not here. Not anymore. This is a chaotic system, ruled by strength and dominance. We no longer need mythic stories to explain our past when we have a geological record.

Faith. It is believing without a good reason. I have no good reason to believe in God. The scientists can find no evidence for God. Life seems too chaotic, too random, too violent to be the handiwork of a loving, creative force. It seems we are all just "Waiting for Godot," and in the end our short lives are dust and ashes in a universe so immense we are incapable of comprehending its size.

I was born in the church and I stayed because I wanted to be assured that my good behavior would insure me against life's bigger pains. I was the best girl. I did all the things right.

I

even

journaled.

I signed letters to my boyfriend, "In Christ."
I went to church in college.
I volunteered for VBS.
I led a Bible study.
I took hymnology.

I fasted
    and prayed
        and cared
            and wrote
                and talked
                    and sang in the choir
                        and still my kid died.
The world I built crumbled. Bad things don't just happen to bad people or good people. Bad things just happen. Really, really crappy things that everyone hates that aren't good for anyone. And the only reason you can bear what God gives is: your heart won't stop beating for a simple thing like grief. Sugar? Apparently. But not grief. A broken heart beats and beats until you find yourself with bruises on your forehead and sad eyes.

It beats until you are face down under a rainbow on a sandy beach that was once the side of a mountain, alone in the world, waiting for the waters to reveal the handiwork of God. The rotting stench of the destruction of every living thing God has ever created except you and your family and a zoo boat.

You are alone in a cave with the sun going down over the dreadful water and your voice is hoarse from screaming. You are standing on the edge of the primordial waters and all you can see is chaos. There is no God-schema that fits this kind of destruction. This is disaster. You will bury the dead in the dead earth and one day die and rot. So, you get drunk because, when you do, at least the prismatic sky seems beautiful. You strip yourself naked and claw your way into the dead earth and tear it with your teeth. You eat great mouthfuls of it trying to stop the flesh-pounding beating of your heart. You choke on the vengeful mud and your fingers bleed, but they? they are still there, rotting beneath the sparkling waves, and you? you are still here, alive enough to bleed.

And what do we tell our children as we hold up our colorful pictures of paired animals and the blue robed Noah? "God loves you, children. When the great flood came, God took care of Noah and his family. And if you obey God, God will take care of you." Bullshit.

Is God? Honestly, when I see the torn hearts of addicts, the generational pain of injustice, the blank stares of media-stupefied masses, I can't find much evidence for God. People live and die in poverty so abject that if there is a God and they ever meet God, they will probably spit on God. But it's not God's fault, you say, God left the church as God's hands and feet.

Then God is a cripple.

So, do I reject the idea that God is and embrace that the world is a chaotic system softened by morality and love but only for those who can afford it? Surely to believe in a Creative force is to willingly believe the unbelievable. A quaint set of superstitions spun like a web of shining sugar to keep us pacified.

Can I stand at the edge of the receding waters with Noah and worship a God of destruction or inattention? It is so much easier to say that there is no God. The earth is a chaotic system of geothermal accidents that sometimes remind people that they are not the gods they think they are. I do not want to believe that a Creator would choose to drown souls, distinct and unique, even if that particular Creator was supremely frustrated.

Noah and I still stand there at the edge of the ossified pool. We have turned away countless times, but each time we do something catches our eyes. There are ripples on the surface of the water. There is something there. Something invisible and deniable. Something profound and wild. Unknowable. Something in the space between the particles of the nucleus that is infinite. More song than prose.

Alien.

Slowly I slip my fingers into Noah's. The sky is stretched with a golden sunset and the water turns to a gilded shroud. If God, then what? If God, how do we live through poverty, hatred, death, and abuse? If God, how do we face centuries of brutality and shaming? It would be easier to go to brunch and forget.

After all, there is no evidence.

And omelets are delicious.

CHAPTER 6

Powerless

I HIT THE STEERING wheel with the palm of my hand while tears soaked into the neck of my shirt. I wasn't the only one with tear-stains on my face.

She brought chocolate candies with the news. Our new neighborhood did not allow farm animals of any kind—especially poultry, and there had been a complaint. The rules must be followed.

We broke the rules. It says so. The properties are deed restricted. No poultry. Not even two. Not even if they belong to a child. Not even if they have names.

"There has been a complaint," she said turning her shoulder so she could get through the door I hadn't quite opened for her. "I waited to come talk to you until after the holidays. I wanted you to have a nice Christmas."

"Oh," I said. "Is there a problem?"

I was wondering if she could have known just how hard Christmas was for me.

"No, well, do you have chickens?"

"Yes. We have two."

"I brought the Homeowner's Association covenant to show you."

She shuffled back through pages of micromanagement regarding the proper height of a fence and what you may or may not park in your driveway.

"Chickens aren't allowed."

She was babbling and twisting the rule-book in her hands. It was uncomfortable.

My children sagged, weeping, onto the floor with the shiny, foil-wrapped candies in their fists. It was a bribe.

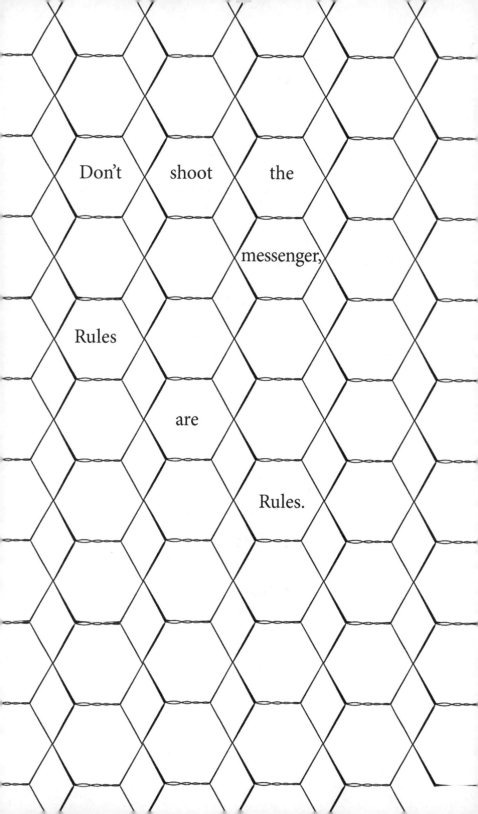

Don't shoot the messenger,

Rules

are

Rules.

I wrote a letter to the committee. I spoke with the president. I raged and cried and shook my tiny fists. And in the end, I packed up my chickens, Elsa and Anna, one small wiry White Leghorn and a fat Rhode Island Red whose legs were bleached white from her long life of egg laying, put them in a box and drove them to a friend's farm.

Annabel, who was four years old at the time, loves chickens. It sounds weird unless you have ever had them. Chickens are bewitching. There is something about the way they do everything that they are supposed to do. They scratch and peck, and at night they roost. They lay eggs and cackle about it. They are soft as down and light as feathers.

Annabel scavenged strawberry tops and watermelon rinds from our kitchen and ran them out to her chickens. She could catch them if they got loose. She knew how to carry them safely. Although keeping chickens was new to me, when the rule book arrived, she did not remember a time without at least two hens in a backyard coop.

Annabel wears dresses, the fluffier the better. She is a glitter-bottom from way back. Her little legs would churn beneath layers of tulle as she ran from our back door to the coop, her golden hair white in the sun and sequins shining. She would open the egg door and scoop out two eggs, one white and one brown. Back inside, eggs and hands washed, then into the pan and onto the plate. She can crack and season and stir all by herself.

I couldn't save them for her.

My words, my arguments, my tears were powerless to protect

my baby from disappointment.

Where were you, God, when I was powerless to save?

When the life in my womb died, I didn't even know. I had to have a machine tell me my baby was dead. I didn't drop her, I didn't forget to give her her medicine, I didn't leave her unattended. I was simply powerless to save her. Perhaps that is why the death of the unborn seems like such a betrayal of the Divine. This life, this person, this daughter whom you love more than you love yourself, more than God asked you to love anything, is out of your control. I did everything I could to keep her safe, I even worried about using the microwave, but, when she stopped moving, I didn't even know that last nudge was her last. I could do nothing. I couldn't even hold her hand or tell her that I loved her. Even one time. Now I am left with a picture and a box and the terribly heavy "why" that will never be answered.

There is no way around this why. There is no road that does not leave you crazy except for the one straight through this why. The little room they gave us after I delivered Gwyneth and was waiting for all the necessary checks to be made before I could go home wasn't in the post-partum area. They gave us a room sort of down the hall in a corner, well away from the sounds of crying babies. Our visitors didn't bring balloons or flowers. They weren't smiling.

One of our friends came to our room sweating sorrow, and, as we embraced, he didn't say congratulations and I didn't say thank you. I said I was afraid of the anger that I knew would come.

I didn't want to be angry. That's not how I wanted to respond to my baby's birth. I didn't want it to expose all the holes in my faith. I didn't want my anger to flare up and burn those I love, for I knew the anger of the powerless must burn hot, fueled by impotence and shame.

You might not think that a still-birth gives rise to shame. I didn't drink or smoke or do drugs or go in for weekly x-rays, but still I felt ashamed. I was the life support and the baby died.

At one of our churches, the first week of every month we sing a call and response song of repentance. It is one of my favorite parts about going. To hear my voice blending with my children's voices and the voices of business executives and addicts in a cry of confession is a place of rightness.

The first time we joined in this song after Gwyneth died, I wept in shame. It was as if a self I was unaware of was confessing to deep darkness.

Infanticide.

Me and Herod. United by shame. The deep, dark shame of an infant's blood.

Part of me was shocked and horrified. I wasn't guilty of anything. Was I?

Am I?

How dare my self take that on? How dare I blame me?

But if not me, whom, still blind mind you?

There is a very familiar and very strange story in the Gospels about Jesus's friend, Lazarus. Lazarus gets sick and his sisters run to tell Jesus—who is neck-deep in miraculous healing stories.

"Hey, guys. You remember that time I spit in the dirt and rubbed it on that blind guy's eyes. He didn't know whether to thank me or punch me."
"Yeah. I remember that one. Then when you sent him to wash, you totally pointed. I am so glad he couldn't see the look on your face when you realized what you did. That was a good day."

Jesus was in the miracle business, and Lazarus was Jesus's good friend. The Gospel writers say that Jesus loved this family. But when Jesus gets the news his beloved friend is desperately ill he says something about how Lazarus isn't going to die from this but

God will be glorified. Then he just sits around for two more days before walking over to check things out. It's weird. Here are three people who are your friends in a sea of faces who all want to touch your magic robe and get a free meal, and when these friends need you, you just mumble something about hypochondriac Jews and cool your heels for two days.

Jesus knew he was going to raise him from the dead. Apparently, that was the plan. Let him get good and dead before you get there to maximize the amount of glory brought to the Father. But then after all the set-up, when Jesus got to the tomb, knowing that he was about to raise Lazarus from the dead for all kinds of important reasons, Jesus stood there and, in the scripture's shortest verse, wept. He cried. He just stood there, in front of everyone, with tears all over his face and ugly cried. He knew the happy ending, but he stood there and blew snot bubbles.

And my question is why?

Why did he cry?

Was it empathy or dust?

Why, when Jesus knew he was going to raise Lazarus from the dead, did he take time to weep?

Perhaps Jesus, the man with dusty feet, felt betrayed. He had just a few friends that would sit and let him eat without seasoning all his food with religious examination. Lazarus, Mary, and Martha had one of the few homes that Jesus is recorded to have stayed in, and yet God wouldn't let him have one friend without using him to make a point. When Jesus stood there in front of Lazarus's tomb, making the dust into mud, I imagine he wanted to hit God the Father in the ear.

Yes, good did come out of it, but couldn't God have found some other way? It isn't as if anyone actually understood. Couldn't God have diverted those little germs somewhere else? A little Divine preventative health care. Mary and Martha were the A-team of disciples and what did they get in return? Two days of inaction and a weeping Jesus. A savior who stood there in front of the tomb of his friend and wept because, perhaps, he was tired of having to make every moment, every relationship, poignant. Couldn't God have saved this one, for me?

CHAPTER 7

And Yet

I AM STANDING IN a cold, clear mountain stream, my words and frustration and anger stripped away, and I am left, quiet and empty, listening to the song of the water gurgling over the stones. God and I call a truce for an afternoon. I am not convinced. I have not given in, but for a moment or a day, I stand soaking in the impossible beauty. Around me, my children are heaving the heaviest rocks they can lift over to the deep pools and dropping them in, shouting with glee at the subsonic "whoomp" and skittering away from the bone cold water that splashes up even though they are already drenched. Their carefree shouts cannot dispel the magic of this place.

In quiet, muddy patches, little periwinkle butterflies sit in groups filling their tiny bodies with minerals and dainty sips of water. Exercising more restraint than is likely healthy, I resist waving them up into a cloud of purple flowers. I wonder if they are always so silent or if they are hushed by my intrusion. Their wings, tidily folded up like a dozen tiny sailboats, wave in a tiny breeze. Perhaps it is my breath that disturbs them. I will watch them for one more minute and then leave them to their silent lives.

A copper headed, rawboned boy of five, without so much restraint, splashes up and whirls, arms outstretched in a fluttering cloud of startled joy.

On the bank, ahead of where I stand is a huge dead pine. The perpetual damp has furred it with moss and lichen, and little demilune fungi create a fairy staircase up the right side. It seems to be coated with life in death. Here, in the misty woods, with my feet in water so cold that the summer's heat won't touch me again today, I see the barest edge of hope.

Doubt still clamors in my head.

If injustice . . . . then God?

If poverty . . . . .then God?

If grief . . . . then God?

Questions circling in my mind like autumn leaves caught in an eddy.

Can there be a God if life hurts so much?

I am not sure. It seems improbable. Even with agonizing beauty all around me, God seems unlikely. But perhaps.

I am willing to allow a *perhaps* to form with the misty woods all around me.

CHAPTER 8

In the Name of

IN THE UNITED METHODIST Church, as in many other traditions, at the front of the sanctuary there is an altar area: the Protestant corollary of a Holy of Holies. It is the sacred space where only the robed do dwell.

In the church where I spent my school years, the altar area was raised above the pews by four powder-blue carpeted steps. There is a vibrant stained glass window centered in the wall behind the altar that hung, stole-like, over a brass cross. The altar itself was a rectangular box—about eighty-four by twenty-eight inches—painted white and cordoned off by a brass railing. On the top of the altar there were four candles, six brass offering plates, and a Family Sized Bible. You know the type. Huge things you pull out to read the Christmas story out of, balanced on both knees, and where, if you were so inclined, you could record the marriages, births, and deaths attendant on your family twenty generations deep. This version had a powder blue ribbon sewn into the spine and gilt pages. All in all, this altar was a lovely reminder of our dependence on grace and brass polish.

The brass railing opened in the front and the back to allow access to the altar. The area behind the altar was a sea of sky-blue carpet. The altar guild wouldn't allow anything to be placed between the altar and the cross in our sanctuary. It was their overwhelming sense that the place of holiest worship in our sanctuary should at no time be separated from the cross theologically or spatially.

Christians are people of the cross after all.

There were four Greek letters centered above and below the crossbars: INRI, which stand for Jesus of Nazareth, King of the Jews—the words tacked over his head as he died.

Words that mocked a man, a God, and a people.

You are no one
From nowhere
King of a conquered people.

A conquered people.

A dead King.

I saw that cross every Sunday from first grade until I graduated from high school. We went every, single week. When it snowed, we walked three miles to church (that only happened one time, but I felt super hardcore for doing it). I knew what that cross meant and why it mattered, and I wanted to lay my gifts and talents on that altar because I wanted to live a life that mattered.

At our church, when you reached fifth grade you went through acolyte training and were given the weekly job of processing the light of Christ and the Bible up the center aisle of the church at the beginning of the service and recessing with it at the end. We wore calf-length robes and used candle lighters with long wicks that you could pull down to snuff or edge up as you walked to keep the flame healthy. The proper procedure for processing with the light of Christ was to carry the lighter with the flame up and the bell down. We would march, in tandem, carrying the flame to the four candles towering well over our heads. We were to light the outer candle first and the inner candle second. While the candles were lit, the third acolyte would place the open Bible on the altar. Usually the ribbon was placed somewhere in the Psalms, but, if I processed the Bible, I would look up the sermon scripture in the bulletin and have the Bible turned to the appropriate page.

No one ever read out of that Bible.
But it seemed like the
Right thing to do.
Just in case.

When I was in fifth and sixth grades, I carried the Light of Christ into the eleven o'clock worship service most Sundays. There was one stretch when I acolyted for sixteen weeks straight. I could replace wicks. I knew the best time to begin the recessional so that we wouldn't delay the benediction or stand, awkwardly, through the last verse of the final hymn. The acolytes sat up in the chancel area tucked behind the pastor and the organist. There were many

Sunday mornings when I would slip down beside the organist and help her turn the absurdly wide pages of her music.

I was, after the example of Paul, an acolyte among acolytes.

In sixth grade, I knelt around those candles and pledged my faith and loyalty to the United Methodist Church. The thin brass railing stayed cool under my white gloves as the pastors laid their hands on my head and repeated the Rites of Confirmation. My blonde hair hung to my waist and my freckles crowded together as I smiled, both proud and burdened to be a full member of the Church.

Now I was a

"Member."

Until that moment, I had simply been an,

"Attends Regularly."

Eleven years later, I knelt at that same altar and pledged an oath to God and to a Man. When I rose that time, I was a member of a new family. A family a boy and I had decided to create. The Family Bible was on the altar. I had turned the page to 1 Corinthians 13.

I had no idea what it meant to live with faith, hope, and love.

Four years later I stood in front of a different altar with two candles, two steps, red carpet, and a wooden railing. My husband, sporting a newly acquired beard and flaxen clerical robe, held the tiny form of our three-week-old son. Our families, who filled about a third of the pews, jammed into the chancel with us as water poured from large hands onto a tiny head.

"In the name of the Father."

The sound of the water was

small

but so powerful.

"And the Son."

I stood wondering what I should do with my face.
Should I cry?
Should I smile?

"And the Holy Spirit."

And it was done.

We had
baptized our
first child.
He screamed
through the
whole thing,
and his head
was as red
as his fuzzy
hair.

About two years before that, in the throes of Divinity School, Luke and I began to debate the finer points of baptism. And then we began to argue. I had a collection of opinions; he had Randy Maddox. I, being a "Sinner in the Hands of an Angry God" (Jonathan Edwards) and concerned about not remembering or consenting to my Baptism, felt like a significant marker of my faith was somehow invisible to me. And I *needed* a marker. A safety net over the abyss. A muzzle for Cerberus. If you got this thing wrong, there would be hell to pay because God was angry. I wanted our children to be baptized when they could ask—a believer's baptism. Proof of atonement because they were, or would be:

sinners.

He, Luke, the boy-turned-man that I married, insisted that baptism was a means, a conduit, of grace, freely bestowed.

But that implied something I didn't understand, after all I was living with Noah's God.

That implied something more universal and unpredictable.
That implied something wild and uncontrollable.
That implied that my answers might not have questions.

At the very least, his God was in much better control of the anger inherent to being a parent.

It was raining. Luke and I were in our car. He was driving and I was weeping. I needed to get this right. It was important. I knew the space in front of the cross was sacred, and I knew baptism had something to do with that.

You must be born again.

We are all nurtured in an aqueous womb. There in the warm, darkness of our mother's body we live as creatures of water. We are merfolk.

I had a recurrent dream when I was growing up that I could breathe water. Not just breathe while under water, I could inhale the thick, cool water deep into my lungs and it made me feel powerful. I could arc and twist like a sea lion. I was beautiful and strong and fast. In that dream, I could return to my primal state when the elemental water flowed through me, but, it turns out, one good wave in the face dispels that dream. Now, when I return to the water-world, grown alien and dangerous, I am condemned to standing on the shore looking out at the unbroken, water-meets-air horizon, grieving at being tossed aside by the maternal water.

I grieve for what was; rejected by the very state where I began. I grieve that when I took that first, rebellious breath, leaving behind my mother's watery womb, I became separate from her. I no longer breathe through her body. I grieve that I have lost Eden.

Isn't that at the heart of this story?

I have lost Eden.

I have been kicked out of the place where good behavior necessarily begets good results. I stand, looking back into the lush, green garden contemplating the relative merits of leaping the flaming swords versus a baseball slide in from beneath. But what if that which I am seeking, the God of before, isn't behind the angelic sentries. What if the garden, like the tomb of Jesus, is empty?

When he was three, Laine was terrified of baptism. I am not sure why, but he would loudly protest baptism, no matter where we were. Even in church. Charming trait in a pastor's kid.

In one of my college classes on religion, we talked about the historic and theological meanings of baptism. We sat, hunched in sage-green plastic chairs, and debated the correlations between the rite of baptism and ancient rites of sacrifice. We postulated about the ramifications of basing religious rites on symbolic death (baptism) and cannibalism (Eucharist) and read articles photocopied landscape-wise, highlighting them in pink and green and yellow and

never

once

wept.

We talked about the Jewish sacrificial laws and how, when Christians claim that Christ is the fulfillment of that law, we attest, without flinching, that we are accepting a religion founded on human sacrifice. We wrote three to five double-spaced pages, in 12-point Times New Roman, about how baptism represented drowning and resurrection and I never even thought to cover my face in horror.

When three-year-old Laine heard of our intention to baptize his, then, six-month-old brother, Oliver, he howled and wept. He was furious that we, his loving parents, would risk his infant brother. How did this boy, only tentatively out of diapers, know the nature of this barbaric act?

How did I go through with it?

Being from water, I return to it. Once again standing in a small mountain river, my feet in water so clear it is invisible until a water skate walks, impossibly, on its surface, I can feel ten thousand years of story eddy around my toes.

Rocks, smooth and brilliant, nestle in the elbows and knees of the river. Tree branches arch overhead creating a mandala of air and water and mist circumscribed in green. Today this water is here passing gently through this wood, but it will soon drain away to another place. Water is ancient. It has cycled through ages and seasons. It has known the splash of children's fingers, the cleft of the explorer's prow, the joy of the thirsty wanderers, and it remembers the shadow of the Divine breath in the darkness before there was light when it, too, knew the darkness and safety of a womb.

Through my curtain of tears, I finally listened. Baptism is not a rite of death and resurrection. Baptism is a rebirth into a life of grace. Baptism is not the work of the person, but the work of God that began before water ever bathed the feverish face of the Earth. This was something mysterious and wild and, yes, a bit dangerous.

I followed the raindrops, full to the brim with reflected worlds, as they slid in streaks along my window. Perhaps these drops had been in the Jordan River on that day when Jesus plunged his head into this mystery. I had had enough of death and sorrow for one day. Perhaps baptism could be about life. Perhaps it could be a sacred mystery through which we join in the life of Christ.

Who wouldn't want that for their baby?

My birthday is in June, making June my birthday month. In North Carolina, in early June, fireflies crawl out of their subterranean burrows, drawn by the need to find each other and in celebration of my birthday. Obviously. They wink and flash, bobbing upward, looking for and knowing each other and filling the warm air with magic. In the brief darkness of a summer's night, the trees fill with the joy and mystery and love of these tiny, trusting bugs.

I am surrounded by the nature of God, but, it turns out, I don't seem to know it very well at all. God has endowed the dirt under my feet with grace so thick sometimes it bursts into light. I was not created in wrath. I was created in love. And yet, surely, in the descent into the waters of baptism, there is a moment of terror. Who can stand before this God who has demanded blood? This filicidal God?

Will I find grace?

The risk of the waters is real. I long to return to the aquatic life of the womb, but now the water holds death for me. I fear that I have been forgotten by the Creator. Perhaps my descent into the waters will go by unnoticed and I will simply drown, condemned to death by the indifference of my God, or, worse, I will simply regain my footing and walk out of the water unchanged.

Will I find grace?

But, risking all, I come, dry and thirsty, to the waters of baptism, knowing that to stand at the edge, weighing the cost, would deny the mystery of the Creator. These waters, ancient and immediate, still ripple with the passing of the Spirit, so I step in.

Will I find grace?

CHAPTER 9

Prayer, Part 1

I NEVER NOTICED HOW many people insist that prayer got them through tragedy until they all told me. But, considering that I was still sitting in a deck chair complaining about God with my friend Noah, I figured I wasn't really in the black with God. I felt like a kid who has dragged bedtime out for three hours who suddenly needs a Band-Aid. Probably I should just stick that bloody thumb in my mouth and wait it out.

Sure, I want other people to pray for me. In the weeks immediately after Gwyneth's death, flocks of people would tell me that they were praying for me. I told them not to stop. I hoped they wouldn't stop, but I couldn't pray for myself. I still can't. Not real evangelical, standing-in-the-gap prayer. I was afraid if I closed my eyes and folded my hands, they would become fists. When I tried, my head would fill with doubt and so many questions. Then I would start remembering all the times that we had prayed and life still hurt.

I was filling up my dog's bowl with water when word came that Uncle Dennis's tumor was benign. Originally they had said glioblastoma multiformae, but perhaps not. Our prayers were working. We had done it! We had managed to swing the hammer and ring the bell, and God answered. Halleluiah! A few months later, Uncle Dennis died of a decidedly unbenign glioblastoma multiformae brain tumor.

Before Uncle Dennis died, I remember visiting him in Kansas. My dad, my dad's sister, and my dad's brother, all together with their children, gathered in peaceful protest: a family sit-in against cancer. All the parents, grandparents and cousins gathered in desperation and reconciliation in a very brown living room. I remember brown carpet and a brown couch and brown paneled walls. It was the second time I remember us all being together.

All the parents were exhausted. The strain of managing illness and children had worn them down to silhouettes. I remember my brother practicing headstands and everyone laughing for one crystal moment as a skinny eight-year-old boy crashed sidewise to the floor.

My dad sat on the brown couch next to his brother who was sprawled out on the recliner, eyes closed, sleeping through the pain of aggressive brain cancer. It was the first time I remember seeing my dad cry.

The tears each fell for a different reason:

disappointment,

regret,

anger,

grief,

hope,

fear,

loss.

There was a family next door whose dog had had puppies. In the way of children, we gathered together and begged to keep one. Russell and Lauren would be taking her home, but we all begged for that puppy like Jesus in the garden. For an hour, we begged and pleaded for that tiny, furry life. Her name would be Maggie and I am sure I promised to take my turn walking her. We got the puppy. She was brown. She was a great dog. It was the last time I saw Uncle Dennis.

I suspect I misunderstand the nature of prayer. For most of my life, prayer was basically begging God for a puppy. Heal the tumor, fix the marriage, change the problem. Right after Gwyneth died, while my body coursed with hormones designed to nurture and nourish a baby, I begged. My mind continued to beg as I slept, dreaming of finding babies in baskets. Maybe there was a baby with a mother who was an addict and couldn't manage to feed and raise her baby. I could give the mother a place to heal and find health while I nourished and cared for her baby.

That's a great idea! Let's do that one, God. Please. *I will do anything.*

I walked through the scenarios in my mind and heart.

I promised everyone and everything I could deal with a damaged baby. I could love a baby no one else wanted. You would never hear me complain. Even in the middle of the night. Because, you see, I had complained. Gwyneth was my fourth baby in five years. I was tired. I knew how babies happened, but I had sought comfort in the arms of my husband on a night when another grief had struck. There had been a death, and, out of my sorrow, we created a life. But when I found out I was pregnant with my fourth baby, I cried. I sat at the top of those stairs that would haunt me nine months later, and I cried. I cried because I was exhausted.

So, the sorrow became guilt
and the guilt
became
prayer.

Dear God,

Please give me my baby back. I will be good. I will love her.

I promise.

But no baby, no mother, no God ever showed up.

My broken-hearted mantra went like this:

I didn't mean to complain.
I could have loved you.
I didn't mean to complain.
I was so tired.
I could have loved you.
Even if you had been sick.
I didn't mean to complain.

And I didn't mean to complain. But when you have four babies in five years your body begins to shout. Loudly. A tremendous terrified clishmaclaver of worry fretted around in my brain. I suddenly understood how women died having children. When Gwyneth died, all the moments I had spent feeling overwhelmed came rushing back like a pendulum of accusation.

You should have rested more.	I could have loved her.
You should have prayed more.	I could have loved her.
You should have complained less.	I could have loved her.
You should have been grateful.	I could have loved her.

Through this whirl I heard a tiny sunshine-yellow voice whispering gently in my heart.

"Can you love me like this?"

That was not the prayer I was praying. I was not praying for peace or absolution or understanding.

I was asking for a baby.

A baby who died, whom I would never dress or feed. My milk and prayers dried up leaving me empty and sagging, but still, the answer remained.

"Can you love me like *this*."

Yes.
I can.
I have had to learn how to be the parent of a dead child.

CHAPTER 10

In Remembrance

WHILE I WAS LYING in the hospital bed, with tubes, ironically, connected to my perfectly healthy body, I heard myself say, "At least we will always have communion. At least we will always have communion."

Luke murmured into my hair as I felt his tears dripping onto my scalp. "Yes, we will always have communion." He held my hand and we cried because we knew we would always have this one thing.

I will never dress this child or change her diaper or search for the perfect Christmas present for her, but she is a being endowed with a spirit that did not evaporate.

I CAN STILL FEEL HER NEAR ME.

I can talk with her. I see her face, not as it was on the foot of the hospital bed, stony and perfect, but as she will be at five with bouncy golden curls and laughing eyes. And that is when I know I have a choice to make.

If I choose to live in denial of the Divine,
   I will have to deny the divine
   within myself
   and within all my children
   and she
   will
   truly

                                        die.

Yann Martel wrote a book one day. It was published in 2002. It won the Man Booker Prize. It is a slice of wisdom. I'm hysterical.

In *The Life of Pi* (go back and read those last two sentences . . . see! Hysterical!) Martel drops this line when he is trying to explain why he has told a fantastical story of a boy and a tiger instead of a literal story of a boy and madness:

> [Pi Patel:] "So tell me, since it makes no factual difference to you and you can't prove the question either way, which story do you prefer? Which is the better story, the story with animals or the story without animals?"
> Mr. Okamoto: "That's an interesting question . . ."
> Mr. Chiba: "The story with animals."
> Mr. Okamoto: "Yes. The story with animals is the better story."
> Pi Patel: "Thank you. And so it goes with God."[1]

Once I decided that I would tell my story, complete with tigers and God, then I could feel the pieces of my faith sliding back together in a completely new way. It was as if a new filter had been added to an old, familiar picture. A picture I loved, but had grown accustomed to. I felt like a toddler walking in spring grass for the first time.

---

1. Yann Patel, *The Life of Pi* (Orlando: Mariner, 2001), 317.

I came, once again, to the sacraments, and this time they filled me with wonder.

Communion is the place where all souls brave enough to allow imagination to become faith meet with the saints, visible and invisible, to share in a joyful, raucous meal.

I will never lose her completely.

I believe, more firmly than I believe in the planet Neptune, that when I go to the communion table Gwyneth is there too. Probably she has dripped juice down her chin. This sacred, ordinary meal of bread and juice is the one table where my whole family can gather. Our Great Thanksgiving of fistfuls of bread dunked in juice.

WE WILL ALWAYS HAVE COMMUNION.

What is it about bread? Gandhi taught that wheat was hope for the poor. It contains protein and carbohydrate and vitamins and fiber. If his people were given the power of wheat, they could survive. A little dirt, a few seeds, a stone to grind it and a fire to bake it, and the body has what it needs.

I love the romance of the garden: the seasons, the hope, the joy of each spring full of possibility and free of mistakes. The practicalities elude me—completely—but the romance remains.

Once, I managed to grow two and a half pounds of soft white winter wheat. I sowed with Divine abundance. The vivid green blades echoed my enthusiasm. The heavy, swollen grain heads grew proudly as if they knew they were a living parable. As I crouched behind the lens of my camera, I could hear their whispered wind-words, spoken with tongues of grass, telling of wood-rough hands that rolled wheat and taught a world to love. As they dried to a pale mustard-yellow they began to shout. Impatient, dry voices rattled their story of passion and loss and renewal.

Never has wheat been so adored. Never so often photographed. Never so lovingly (or unconventionally) threshed and winnowed. For this—this simple, nutritious seed, connected me to the soil and to the God who first scattered seed and to the man who came and told its story.

Warm, soft, whole; love wrapped in stoneware. I make the loaves two at a time, mixing and kneading, stretching and shaping until the heat freezes the gluten sheets billowed with the final breaths of the yeast. For me, homemade bread is the joy of a mother's deep knowing that her children are fully fed, completely nourished and tenderly satisfied. In a moment, the whole will be cut into cinnamon sugar toast, peanut butter and jelly, and grilled cheese, but, now, while the fragrant heat slips silently into memory, this humble creation of water and wheat stands as a symbol of home and family and faith.

One loaf made and broken again and again, giving each body the elements of life and each soul the vitalizing gasp of hope. This silent loaf, two pounds, lunch, joins the disparate and time-flung souls and bids them remember the hands that took up bread and a story and gently changed the world. Those hands, just beginning to show age, selected the humblest of foods to hold in remembrance the simple, mothering Divinity. A new way and an enduring love, both needing a metaphor. A metaphor of seed and growth and home and nourishment. An alchemy of grain into sustenance and love into hope.

As a woman, I understand seasons and cycles. My body waxes and wanes like the tides, moon, and seasons. A monthly revolution between life and death, rest and industry, nourishment and decay. Each spring, I fling out hope in seed form, knowing from the depths of myself that to come through the seasons of darkness you must invest faith in the light, and that to see the light as light, you must be willing to walk straight through the darkness. One might say through the valley of the shadow. The dark days must follow and be followed by the light.

To tell of the light, without telling of darkness, tells only half the truth. In my deepest sadness, I needed to hear that there was light. But, when the shock wore off I needed to be in the darkness. There is fullness to walking through the darkness.

WITHOUT DARKNESS, LIFE HAS NO SHAPE.

This is the gift of the darkness.

WITHOUT LIGHT, LIFE HAS NO FOCUS.

This is the gift of the light.

Each autumn, I look out at the withered ruins of the seeds I sowed in the spring and feel despair.

What once was will never be again.

We are ruined by cold, short days. The vibrant green of the summer has faded to translucent browns and yellows. Decay is nibbling at the edges of everything—even our memory. But soon, very soon, we see green pushing its way back up through the dirt. Suddenly we realize that the fatigue of the autumn has given way to expanse and hope.

Foolish, foolish hope.

Maybe this year will be different.
Maybe this year I will harvest something.
Maybe this year will bring plenty.

I dream of the year that my canning shelves will be full. I dream of the day I can feed the hungry with the fruit of my labor. The cycles of hope, of planting, of growing, of watering echo in my heart. Maybe it is the gift of womanhood or the imprint of the Creator.

Jesus knelt before God and bled his doubt and fear out in prayer, and when he stood and brushed the dry dust and olive leaves from his knees, he stood to face darkness. Night, hate, fear, and failure. How could he have known that the Creator would take his effort and weave the atmosphere of a new kingdom. When Jesus prayed in the garden, he wasn't worried about his scattered disciples or making sure people interpreted the symbology of the cross correctly. Jesus wept. For himself. For the terror of walking into the darkness. This is not an easy road, the road through the darkness.

Grief is painful.

Suffering is painful.

How do you explain God in a world where children die of hunger? How can the God of the Eucharist not be big enough to feed everyone?

I don't know.

Mystery.

But, if there is no God, why do I care? Why do I imagine a world where everyone has enough?

I don't know.

Mystery.

No, light is not all there is, but light gives me direction. I have learned that God is here, in the dark with me, but I can't stay here. I must gather up my things and walk through the darkness and into the light and back around and through each, necessarily, because otherwise life would be flat.

I have no idea why babies die or people are mean or paper cuts hurt so much, but to sit here on a sand pile built of the grains of my broken answers, refusing to move on, unwilling to walk through mystery until my teeth fall out and my eyes cloud over seems a very sad story indeed.

So, without one single reason why, I choose the better story.

CHAPTER 11

Energy

When you have a shared traumatic Experience, people are often driven to tell you their stories. It is mutually necessary.

There is some mystical power in the "Me too" stories. It can be painful to hear his pediatric cancer story or her SIDS story, but isolation is worse. Knowing there are others out there who have found a way to keep breathing means I can do it too.

Most of the time, while you are sharing your stories, the conversation will turn to the things that got them through. Things that had become means of grace to them and now carry all the weight of hope for them. In repeated acts of incredible love and generosity, they handed them all to me—books and CDs and handwritten prayers. Tempting morsels for a soul that had quit eating.

"Oh, thank you. I am sure this will be so helpful." I said.

I never opened them.

I squirreled them all away. I could feel how deeply these things had braced the lives of the givers, but they were just things for me. Even now there is CD with hand-written liner notes in my media basket. VHS home movies, a few CDs from high school, and this mix-tape talisman against despair. I've never listened to it, but I know it's there. Proof in a slim jewel case that I am not alone.

You can tell when someone is coming to talk to you about "hurt." HURT. *HURT!!!* Theirs and yours. They make all kinds of eye contact and start with, "I just wanted to tell you that . . ." My inner eyes would roll while I felt a tremendous hunger for their story. I wanted to shout and stomp and build levies with my broken-answer sandbags and I wanted to curl up and let the words of those who *knew* lave me like crystal blue water on a hot Caribbean afternoon. I needed the stories because they dripped with the energy of the teller, and that energy felt as powerful and necessary as nectar to a bee.

One of the scientific foundations of our understanding of the world is the Law of the Conservation of Energy. I believe this is why parents are so tired. Humans are born with a standard weight of energy that is stolen directly from their parents. The other day, my kids asked me why I walk so slowly. Well, there are lots of reasons for that. But, mostly, they took all my energy.

But spiritual energy must be different. Sometimes when I hear someone's story or tell my own story, I can feel energy flow back into my life. Sometimes I immediately burn it all up as anxiety, but sometimes, on a lovely, good day, that energy sparks life. Just a little bit of golden life daring to blossom on the shore of the flood of sorrow.

I have lived and cried and laughed and raged since Gwyneth died. I desperately want to stay immediately sad forever because grief is my baby's only blanket. To admit healing to any degree is to lose the immediacy of this person whom I love but can barely remember.

Who can remember every detail of their newborn baby? What was is replaced by what is. Behind a parade of new shoes and lost teeth and Disney Pixar movies, the nursing blistered lips and impossibly thin fingernails fade a bit. But for me. For her. There is no what is. There is only grief.

But, unexpectedly, like a beloved blanket, even grief frays around the edges and loses its color, softened by time and washing.

CHAPTER 12

Broken

WHEN NINETEENTH-CENTURY COMPOSER GUSTAV Mahler's five-year-old daughter died, his music changed.

When I scribbled that fact down in my first semester of college I didn't realize the staggering, gasping, choking finality of those words. The death of a child. Of course I didn't. We talked about how you could hear him processing his grief in the music he wrote after Maria died of scarlet fever and diphtheria. His music became more melancholy. Even if you don't know his story, you can hear it in his compositions. An inference about a creator from his creation.

Later, in a whole new set of classes, I was taught that in the body structure reflects function. Teeth that are flat are meant for grinding and teeth that are pointed are meant for ripping and tearing. Perhaps structure also reflects constructor.

Yes, the mystical is inexpressible, but not foreign. I am surrounded by things so extraordinary that they shout of the hand that sketched them from the void. I look at the wet clay vessel on the wheel and find the thumb-print of a great imagination. Yet we are startled by the cracks and broken places. Our certainty of Creator is thrown aside by the certainty of horror: the blood of children enslaved to harvest cocoa beans, the bodies piled up in the corners of the wars over lines in sand, the hate that attacks faithful love.

I fell in love with horses at age seven. I didn't even know it was cliché. I am not sure I would have cared. I talked, read, and dreamt about horses. I wrote stories about them. I drew them over and over and over, and I knew that when I felt the warm huff of air on my cheek, blown from nostrils studded all over with wiry hairs, that this creature breathed the same breath that had hovered over the waters of creation. This noble beast was proof that there had once been Eden. If you have ever looked into the eye of a horse, you know that this eye was born of mystery. They are orbs that hold a power and grace that is very far from tame.

When I was in high school my Sunday school room had cinderblock walls and a bank of north facing windows. The couches were second-hand and pilling. I used to pull off the pills while I was listening and pile them up into tiny little hills of age. Slow motion decay. One morning, my Sunday school teacher closed her lesson with a poem. I was about three piles in. I don't remember what the poem was called or who wrote it. I don't even remember the words, but I do remember what I heard. God made everything to be beautiful on purpose. God creates as a love song. Jewels of fire and gold hung from a tree branch for a week. And we sweep up all of those carefully painted leaves and throw them away. We ignore the gestures of God and then complain that we can't see God.

From that moment, I began searching for the reflection of God in the little bits and pieces of life, noticing the shimmer that means that this thing, right here before you, needs your attention: the reassuring flash of the Divine in a darkened world around me. If there is a God, and if that God created, perhaps that creation reflects the, otherwise, invisible. Perhaps I will find the courage to face the God who does not always calm the storm. I have hidden for a long time sitting on the stairs, hoping that this sense of a lurking Divine will pass like a bout of severe dizziness. It hasn't passed. Instead, I noticed a tree outside the window.

Across the street in our neighbor's yard stands a huge oak tree. I don't know what kind of oak tree. Just a big one. In the winter it is indistinct from all the other trees in the neighborhood, but in the summer it is a partner in my grief. At some point the tree must have undergone some trauma because its foliage does not reach the tips of the branches. My guess is that when the builders of my neighbor's house cut the driveway next to the tree, they must have damaged its root base enough to cause the die-back. There are about two feet of bare limbs exposed beyond the blur of leaves. It is uncomfortable to look at—it's too revealing. The pain of a broken life. Those stark sticks grotesquely scraping the sky. Exposed for all to see. Brutally naked. Abandoned.

When its roots were cut, each tiny fiber sheered by metal teeth, the tree must have shuddered and wept. The tree didn't die though. It felt the pain of death, but did not die. That first winter it didn't know if spring would come for it again. When the dew no longer frosted the grass and the earthworms began their silent revolution, when warmth of spring came and night began to lose its grasp, when the birds returned to its branches and the soil bubbled with sprouts, its leaves budded again, first just a swelling, then squirrel's-ear leaves, then the hands of summer; but the damage left its mark.

Life after tragedy.

Now there is a swing hanging from the lowest branch. A child, with bruised knees and golden curls, flies in repeating arcs, arms splayed in tree-born flight. Her Dada stands behind her soaking in her joy. Laughter drifts up through the leaves to the bare limbs.

Joy after tragedy.

So, I will start here, peering cautiously out, willing to believe. Looking for something ineffable. I am not the same. Life is not the same. God is not the same. But I can feel my soul swelling just a bit. A bud—maybe two.

Hope after tragedy.

CHAPTER 13

Sunrise

I WENT INTO LABOR with my first child at 4:50 a.m. It was dark, I was three days overdue, and 211 pounds. I wanted to have that baby so badly I welcomed the pain that meant he was coming. It was a slow labor. He was very large and it took a long time to get us both ready for birth. It would be forty-two hours before he arrived, purple and screaming.

After a day of labor we entered the darkness. The midwives had instructed me to rest, but I was anxious and excited. I turned on all the lights trying to beat back the night and the rising fear.

Pain and fear and darkness.

We watched a movie called Noise and ate a pizza, which I would throw up later, and tried to go to bed. Our contraction-timing sheet was filling up. I lay in bed, Luke's fists pressing against the pain in my back, staring into the darkness. At 2:00 a.m. Luke fell asleep. I was alone in the dark, and I could feel it wrapping around me like eternity.

The pain and fear and darkness and me.

But that's not fair, is it? Darkness is not malignant. Darkness simply is an artifact of gravity. Our insistent spinning which holds our feet to the dance floor also interrupts the light while we are suspended in our own shadow for the space of a night. Like all things, it must give way to inexorable time.

There are three stages of dawn: astronomical, nautical, and civil. Astronomical dawn is but the lessening of darkness. No hint yet of the nature of the sun, but a promise that this day too will see its rising. This darkest stage of dawn is held in the grip of night. It is but a sign. The night must soon depart, gathering its blanket of darkness around it, making room for the day. Long before the sun itself is visible over the horizon, irrepressible light comes to spoil the surprise of its coming. Soon, the east will reveal itself as we find the shapes of things once more. Lovers must relinquish the mystery of oneness and return to the roles of the day. We are revealed. Again. With the civil dawn, day can no longer be denied. Soon, the sun will break the horizon and those without excuse will rise with it. Come again is the joy of work, the casting of shadows, and the spinning of the world.

I discovered the joy of the sunrise when I lived in Etowah, North Carolina. Etowah is a retirement community with two golf courses, a grocery store, and the best thrift shop you will ever visit. When we lived there we had two, then three kids. I would go into the thrift shop with five extra dollars and come out with yards of fabric from someone's cleaned out stash. Once I walked in and saw, sitting on a table all of its own, a circa 1950s turquoise typewriter. It had a case and type that flew up and stamped the paper, and I bet it had a bell that rang at the end of the line. It was thirty-five dollars. $35. Turquoise is my favorite color. My husband's granddaddy was a typewriter repairman. It was there for me. It was an emblem of the we-ness of us: writers, hand-crafters, lovers of turquoise. I bought a few three-yard rolls of interfacing for seventy cents each and went home to find thirty dollars and seventy cents.

It was gone when I went back that afternoon.

Retirement communities have great thrift stores, but you have to act fast. Some lessons are learned in your body.

In Etowah, we lived on three acres in the middle of seventy acres of corn. From my back porch I could watch the sunrise over rows of corn. The hedge-row of trees on the far end of the field would try to suppress the coming day, but after a moment or two of struggle with the upper branches, the sun would come pouring through in a silent blast of color and light. The cornfield bordered the French Broad river on the south side, so most mornings mist would rise off the water and hover over the fields until after sunrise. Those were the best. The mist would turn gold and yellow in brilliant rays. I felt as if molten light was streaming toward me. I wanted to shout for everyone to come look.

Wake up! This is important.

But I didn't.

Some moments are not for shouting.

A sunrise is set to a wild, cacophonous soundtrack of bird song and lifts its glory moment by moment until it is gone—before the light becomes, simply, day. Filtering through the trees or mountains or lifting out of the sea, day comes on with unstoppable, demanding force. This is the new day.

A sunrise is not a moment or a rigid set of events. The time between night and day is large and spacious. Just as calculus measures the space under an arch with moving estimation, a sunrise is a calculus of time, each moment infinitesimally small, until, in life's greatest anticlimax, it is full day. The shy, slow sunrise evaporates with the dew and its freshness is wilted and forgotten under the crescendo of the day, and when the darkness returns, we pad our nests with the hope of the distant sunrise.

A sunrise is a secret space of joy and hope, a thing that promises that there is more than random chance and suffering, a gentle demonstration that, although we may seek to explain the gravitational power of rotating masses, we are helpless to control them. Somehow, that seems right. A sunrise is a song to welcome the day.

CHAPTER 14

Metaphor

These things: cold rivers, butterflies, dead trees, and light, are, for me, eloquent metaphors for the mysteries of life, faith, and being. Only they aren't just metaphors, they are more like stain for a slide. When a scientist or student wants to examine something with a microscope, he or she will often dye whatever he or she intends to look at. Without the dye everything is hidden in monochromatic fuzz.

Ideally, different parts of whatever is being looked at absorb dye differently, so, ideally, cell walls and mitochondria spring into relief unveiling another world of which we are made.

In biology lab, I remember sitting on a four-legged stool silently losing myself in a world of onion cells vibrantly yellow and amoeba scandalously red. A white lab coat and another world embracing me for an afternoon. One drop of blue or yellow or red and a parallel universe is revealed in a single drop of water.

When I was in school, somewhere around the eighth grade, judging by the handwriting, I began a word journal. A word journal, according to me, is a notebook where I record words that I needed to look up or just liked. Mine was made out of a little spiral bound notebook. I counted out the sheets of college-ruled pages and apportioned them to each letter with little primary colored tabs. I did not divide the paper evenly between the letters but in accordance to the preponderance of words likely to be awarded to it. When I found a word, I wrote it slowly and clearly, wanting, above all, legibility, and then wrote its definition. No annotation. It wasn't a test-prep tool or a study guide. It was just my book of words. Beloved words.

Filed on the page with a green stick-on "H" tab is the word *hermeneutics–n. the science of explaining and interpreting.* At some point in my reading-life, I found this word and stopped long enough to record it. An important word. My soul found meaning in pursuit of the hermeneutics of being. I hope it still does.

It turns out that metaphor is the vehicle of my hermeneutical exploration and my stain to examine the gossamer sheen of faith and God. The faith found in the color of the mourning dove. The God reflected off the surface of still water.

A sunrise is a metaphor. It reveals something of the sublime if I look. Like spilling oil onto a paper with a secret, white-crayon message, I scan the sky for the key to unlock the mystical. Some code for translation. A Rosetta Stone for spirituality. I have done biblical word searches, read commentaries, listened to sermons, sung songs, retreated, and mission-tripped looking for some glimpse of the ineffable. And it was there, but always lurking at the corner of my eye. Never someplace where I could sit and sketch it out; measuring each angle and shape against all the others until it dissolved in my mind and reappeared, in two charcoal dimensions, on my blank page.

Whether or not it is reasonable, skies scrubbed blue after a summer storm, a rose-tinged moon rising in the light of the setting sun, syrup-dripping Maple trees, and yellow-onion cell walls speak to me of life thick with meaning. Sometimes I am too busy to notice, but it's there, just below the surface. The shimmer of grace and hope that promises that each breath I take, each mess I clean up, each tear that slips down my face that no one sees isn't some depressing joke.

For me it is proof that chaos is only part of the story.

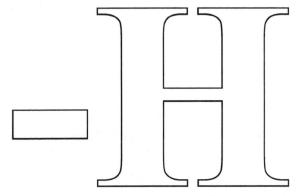

CHAPTER 15

Sunbeam

IN OUR CORNER OF the Western North Carolina mountains it rains a lot. In the summer, the vegetation begins to encroach on civilization, encouraged by the heavy humidity and incessant rain. Stone seems to bud and blossom and the air pearls into something more dense than a gas but, surprisingly, still invisible. On the rare July afternoons when the blue skies elbow the clouds aside, the prune-fingered people emerge from their shelters, squint-eyed and wary. Frequently, a rumor of blue sky is enough to give entombed families courage to squelch out of their doors and fling themselves at the merest wink of blue. After three days of dripping and pouring we saw one slanting finger of light and ran. It was sprinkling just a little when we piled out of our musty minivan onto a muddy, creek-side path. We were not the first desperate venturers. We added our tracks to those already flung over the path. Bike tires, dog pads, shoes. We were all there.

We flowed down to the swollen creek just like all the spontaneous rain-driven rivulets. There was another family already knee-deep in muddy water.

As I often do, I was looking for the shimmer that often meets me in the cover of trees. Something about the muddy banks or the showery skies. Would the universe meet me and supply me with a few more words for my collection? No? Perhaps not today. Perhaps we were just there. Playing. There was no greater truth beyond the truth of family. Feet in the cold water and dodging the splashes of four-year-olds, I settled into a moment just for us. We exchanged pleasantries, played with borrowed toys and laughed at the blue of the sky.

Then other wanderers crested a hill. This time two men and a woman. I felt myself stiffen as I evaluated these new pilgrims. Denim shorts, frayed and smeared with paint and grease, leathery tanned arms, and thickened clubbed fingernails. A polite smile, a meeting of eyes, a return of reserve. These were, like us, seeking the sun, but we were not the same. A quick reapportionment of the sandy creek bank, us here and them there, and we resumed our play. Balance restored. A quick game of tag, an acknowledgment of dinnertime, and we prepared to leave our respite.

But then my daughter broke from my hand and ran to the other woman standing isolated on the creek bank. With a cry of, "Mommy, it's my friend!" she flung her arms around the woman who had been a stranger and other and embraced her as the divine soul she was. Maybe her life wasn't changed by the exuberant love of a child, but mine was. Here was the mystical, breaking out into a cynical and fearful world. An embrace of resurrection.

This is the truth of my life. I must seek to become a person of the sunrise. Living fully through the transition between darkness and light. It turns out that Jesus's call is not just to live in the day but to also embrace the night. A creature of two worlds. The doubt that darkens my life is not just an injury to recover from, it is my chiaroscuro. I am called to be a doubter, like Thomas. Us doubters leave a legacy of being shown what we asked to see, and, if it is not the most blessed route, it is, at least, honest.

Jesus said, "Follow me." Following a king who served and a savior who died is not easy. It is a difficult way. Change. Sorrow. Uncertainty. We are set to follow a man who lived so long ago that the stones he threw into the Sea of Galilee as a boy have worn to sand. We, as followers of this man, are the still-glowing embers of the distant sunrise that broke on the earth when Jesus broke bread and asked us to remember. The sunrise faded for me and disappeared into the shadow of night. That was a difficult place. When my husband walks in shadow, it is difficult to watch. I want everything to be fixed, certain, healed.

But, Thomas put his fingers into holes that had scabbed over.

There was time between death and resurrection.

Time of pain and despair and doubt . . .

These places of sorrow are places of value, not to be rushed out of.

The darkness hurts. We separate the light from the darkness trying to create a distinct realm for each. Happiness is light and good; pain is darkness and bad—but if we divorce light from the dark, obliterating the twilight, we create a life that is false and disappointing. We will never be able to live without pain. Pain is not always a symptom of anything more malicious than being alive.

The average life expectancy in America has increased thirty percent in the last one hundred years. With our octogenarian promise clutched firmly to our deserving breasts, we have grown wary of death. No longer a natural conclusion to life, death is an opponent to be eluded and, ultimately, defeated. Life must be lived in perpetual day.

Lighted.

Caffeinated.

Living.

To be still and quiet, invisible for a time, is to risk death. And we have grown fond of our light and our life.

CHAPTER 16

Now What?

I HAVE COME TO realize that there might be a God and a next step, but I do not see what it is. That's easy, you say. Love God, love others, serve the poor. But I can't. I am exhausted by noon and there is always someone out of underpants and there is so much pain in the world one person is powerless against it.

Religion feels hollow: a once-a-week ritual with free childcare and just enough prepackaged guilt to make it seem real. I can drop the kids off at Sunday School and let my head empty out for an hour and I get to wear my awesome new heels. A place where I go stare at my hired professional religious performer. The choir sings, the plate is passed, I sign the register so I get credit for coming, but perfect attendance didn't insure me against pain.

I have become as fractious as a teething child confronting pain for the first time. It isn't fair. If God is, then why do I hurt so much? I have spent years throwing my own private tantrum, but my time in the twilight has shown me that faith and spirituality is not just a vector—a point with direction—faith is also a place to dwell while our spirit yearns toward the divine; it is a journey with a God who weeps along with Rachel and me.

Luke is an Eagle Scout. When he was thirteen he slept outside more than he slept inside. I have camped too. Six times. Eleven nights. Total. What makes it so hard for me to go camping is that God created me out of flesh, not out of dust, and I hate dust. I hate dust. I hate when dust is on my feet. I hate when dust is on my hands. I consider it to be a very difficult moment when dust gets on my bed. When Jesus said if you are not welcomed in a place, shake the dust off your feet and go on, my soul sang. That is a scripture I can relate to. Shaking the dust off.

Annabel loves bugs. Two of her five birthday parties have been bug themed. She once picked up a baby copperhead snake thinking it was the most awesome worm ever. She wants a stinkbug as a pet. I appreciate the function of bugs. I love worms. I wholeheartedly acknowledge their right to live in their home, nature. I do not particularly enjoy those bugs when they bonk around the inside of my tent perilously close to my face, and I don't like to sleep on the ground or floor because that's the bug highway.

Also, nature is loud. The first time Luke and I went camping we went to Yellowstone on July third. I was raised in central North Carolina. In July the grass gets so dry it is a fire hazard, and it is so hot the grass might go ahead and burst into flame just to cool off. We set up our tent, explored the most fascinating place I have ever been, and worried about bears. We did not worry about the correct thing. We did not worry about it almost snowing. All night long I shivered in my thirty-year-old down mummy bag I had borrowed from my dad. The zipper was broken. I was wearing all my clothes. It rained. Immediately my wilderness-hardened new husband began sleeping the best sleep of his life. The rain thundered down on my head. I think it was doing it on purpose. After the rain lost interest and went off in search of other entertainment, there were about thirty-two minutes of quiet before the birds stretched their delicate wings shook the rain from their shiny little eyes and began screaming. I gave up. Nature hates me.

This surprises me. I have always been on the verge of great adventure. In all the fantasy adventure stories, the heroes and heroines walk all day, cook the meal they caught in their snares, and roll up in their woolen cloaks and sleep the sleep of the righteously brave. Maybe I need a woolen cloak.

I just don't see the point of modern-day camping. It seems absurd to pay hundreds of dollars to take portable versions of everything in your house and go set all of those things up and get them all irreparably dirty then come home and try to clean them after having spent however many nights not sleeping because you forsook your perfectly good bed to go sleep outside.

But I could seriously get behind a quest. I am sure if I had a quest, I would become immune to buggy, dusty, clamorous Nature. When I was ten, reading the autobiography of Bilbo Baggins, I thought life would be an adventure. I thought life would be a journey of purpose. I thought I was brave.

But I am not brave. I am a weak, clean coward. Instead of journeying through the wild and sleeping wrapped in a woolen cloak, I find myself reading blogs about better ways to do laundry. I have no ring of power to destroy. I have 387,498 Legos to tame. I am not a great warrior fighting for the good of all, I am a tidy, re-arranger of pillows.

Faith isn't some grand adventure, and it doesn't keep you safe from life's tragedies. I am not sure exactly what it is about, but it won't let me go. As much as I have tried to quit it, there is something within me that pushes me forward toward my quest, my personal Mount Doom—whatever that is. Tears on my face and no path that I can see, I struggle forward uncertain and filled with doubt. Maybe the question isn't, why did Gwyneth die, but, rather, why am I still alive?

In his podcast episode, *Making Room for the Immensities*, Rob Bell said you cannot go around grief. To heal, you must go through it. But the thing is, sometimes you don't want to heal because the pain is all you will ever have. If I let go of one small part of my pain I am terrified that I will lose my baby. She will slip away from me; driven by my absent-minded laughter.

But if I don't heal, I will be stuck here.

When we first had kids, we went through a series of moves. In six years, Laine lived in six different houses. I remember getting in the car when Laine was a toddler and Annabel was a baby and just driving somewhere to get away from the mess of moving. We moved into a house we would only be able to live in for a few months and tears would come to my eyes when I looked at the stacks of boxes and junk I only had a few minutes at a time to fix. Naptime. Bedtime. I started with my sink. If I could get my sink clear, I could at least make food.

The world can feel like a boxed-up kitchen. The toaster is over there, under the pots and pans and stemware and the blender is buried under a box of mixing bowls and a handful of broccoli rubber bands and it brings you to tears just to think about cleaning it all up. I am so fearful that if I start out to do something I will do it wrong or I won't be able to see it through. I can only just imagine the joy of the tidy counters, perfect for preparing meals for my family. I used to think the Kingdom of God was the clean kitchen. The goal. The perfect end.

But the Kingdom of God is in the process. I hope.

CHAPTER 17

Charlotte

DURING GWYNETH'S FUNERAL, THE organist played Mozart's *12 Variations on Ah! Vous Dirai-je, Maman* (Twinkle, Twinkle Little Star). It was beautiful. I stopped being sad just for a moment, proud of having picked such an appropriate and lovely song. Seems strange, but it was the only party we will ever throw for her, and I am glad we had lovely music.

"Why did Charlotte die?" Her words were husky and soft, and she was wiping her soft girl-cheeks. Gentle tears shed for a spider from a story. *Charlotte's Web*, a simple story of friendship and hope and death and birth written for children and to amuse the author.

"Charlotte died because spiders don't live very long."

"But I think it is sad for her to die," said Annabel.

"It is sad, but it's not wrong."

The cycle of life is to live and die and it is sad but it's not wrong. As a westernized society, we have insulated ourselves from death so absolutely that death now seems grotesque. I have vaccinated my children and get the flu shot every year and don't eat trans-fat and exercise—all to keep death at arm's length.

The death of one of my children has connected me inescapably with mortality and it looks entirely different to me now. There isn't a day that I don't consider how fragile life is. Sometimes I have my hands clenched around all of our days, hoarding them and furious that I might be asked to share one of them, but other times I know that there is something beyond myself, something that beckons me to leave the shrouded corner and know that death and grief are not the end of my story or hers.

Christianity has done a strange thing to the life and purpose of Jesus Christ. We have been told that the Kingdom of God is heaven. We are not beings of earth, we are just here for a moment before we are transported to the eternity of our choice. That can't be right! That makes these years simultaneously worth everything and nothing.

I am still wrestling with my conception of heaven. When my children ask about it, I have to admit that I just don't know because I have never been there. No, I don't know how you get there. No, I don't know where it is. No, I do not understand. But, I can feel that my baby is there.

When Gwyneth was born, her grandmothers washed her body and dressed her in a baptismal gown. I couldn't do it because I couldn't stand. When they handed her to me, in the only outfit she would ever wear, I searched my heart for room for this. I had made room for all my children, and I would for this one too.

I remember looking at my husband, whose face had gone all wrong, and stroking his beard. It was soft and wiry and pressed back against my hand assuring me that we were both real. Unfortunately. We would have to make room for this too.

I haven't precisely accepted death. I cried when Charlotte died too, but only because death hurts in a place so deep tears are its only voice. I am not over it, but it isn't wrong. We are born to die just like the grass and the flowers. The flower must fade before it becomes a seed, and I envy it its purpose in death. We must die only because we cannot live forever. On October 16, 2013, my world ended. It was not the first time the world has ended.

In 1348 the bubonic plague killed one third to one half of Europe or between seventy-five and two hundred million people.

It was the end of the world.

In 1918, between twenty and forty million people died of influenza.

It was the end of the world.

In 2004, a tsunami in the Indian Ocean killed over two hundred and thirty thousand people. 230,000. Killed by a wave.

It was the end of the world.

In 2013, a child died.

It was the end of my world.

You don't have to conjecture about end times. Time has ended a thousand million times. Things too brutal to be swept along with time jam up the gears and a person is ejected from time into the end of what makes sense. A place where grief is the only language and shock is the atmosphere you breathe.

"Why did Charlotte die?"

Charlotte died because that is what spiders do, but what Wilbur did was make her brief life visible. I don't know what to do about grief and loss. But even I can make the least of these visible.

I will stop and look into the face of my child when he is howling in terror for the seventh time today because there are monsters—it is to the little children that the Kingdom is given. I will stop and read real stories about friendships and death even when there is cereal glued to my granite countertops because those are the things that matter. I will pause and listen to a lispy three-year-old tell me something important so that when his world ends, he won't have been invisible.

I can't keep the world from ending. I can't stop the wars or the plagues or the disasters. I can't fix grief and loss, but I can refuse to let them be invisible. The only thing God ultimately asks of us is to love God and love those he packs in around us.

The problem is, when we love, our hearts will be broken by it.

There is a place on the Blue Ridge Parkway where my husband and I watched the ashes of our daughter blow away. The mountains were burning with the colors of fall and the sky was strikingly blue. Carloads of people wielding lenses and pausing to embrace the brisk beauty passed by. We saw the beauty too. A beauty in ashes. She was beautiful. A perfect mouth, cheeks soft and round, peach fuzz hair. It made me sad for her to die. My world ended for a collection of moments.

It made me sad, but it was not wrong. She just didn't live very long.

The life I want is impossible. I want the world to be a simple place where there isn't a neighbor who needs my jacket, where children don't die, where it is more sinful to hate your neighbor than skip church. That's the life I want.

Does God want me to stretch out my arms and embrace God's abundance? Of course, but the one thing that I always forget is that God considered manna scattered like dew while God's people were lost in a desert to be abundance.

CHAPTER 18

Winter

HERE IN WESTERN NORTH Carolina, in our comfortable mountains, snow is rare. If more than two inches fall, it is a reason to cancel scheduled programming and layer on anything warm and waterproof we can find, line our un-insulated rain boots with warm socks and plastic grocery bags, dig out the purple plastic sled we found in the garage but no one remembers buying, and hurl our oddly bundled bodies onto rain's much more magical cousin. Once removed, but still definitely water. After all of the snow is tasted and rolled in and trampled on and soaked through our mismatched gloves, we squish back inside where reddened toes and cheeks will thaw by the gas logs. After these truly memorable twenty-two minutes, winter becomes day after day of wind and cold and bare tree limbs. Huddled under layers of wool, I remember the green wild of our rainy mountain summers. The air thickens with damp so tangible you feel as if you need to push it aside as you walk. Plants evade any effort to tame and manicure them, overwhelming the sidewalks under a tide of tangled growth. There are fifteen hours of light and no pile of coats on the van's floorboards. Viewed from here, those summer days seem an extravagant time. Easy living. Of course the mosquitoes and mowing are forgotten as we spend the dark nights inside dreaming of lemonade and cucumbers.

A tree's rings are made by the periodic nature of its growth and rest. All of nature seems to be punctuated by the same. High tide and low. Summer and winter. Life and death. But as a parent, winter and rest seem, respectively, eternal and fabrication. I am faced with days full of restless energy and what feels like an utter lack of accomplishment. I will never, never feel rested again and yet, I am restless and unquiet.

Tired and fevered.
Fatigued and antsy.
Unsettled.

I rustle from window to window, watching the red and gold of autumn fade to grey. Suddenly, all the trees stand exposed, defiantly shirking their responsibilities as lovers of light and air and shade and rattling through their season of rest. Nothing can induce them to forego their slumber. They know better. Winter is one bird's singing. It is cold and dark and meaty.

Broomsedge is a tasteless, worthless weedy grass. It doesn't demand rich or aerated soil. It grows in the left-over patches. Bumping over a well-grazed pasture in central North Carolina in an unclassically antique pick-up truck, a life-long dairy farmer pointed to a line of knee-high broomsedge all gone to seed. It looked like spray from a leaky hose.

"That means I left the liming off too long," he said.

I probably nodded. I probably had nothing to add. I had no idea what he was talking about.

For some reason, I remember those feckless weeds, un-palatable to grazing animals, standing golden and nodding. Broomsedge has little to offer pastured animals, being almost devoid of nutrients and, apparently, taste, so it stands, unmolested, alone. Winter's golden mantle, it washes down the sides of pastures like a fool's-gold river exposed by the greyness of winter. In the drab quiet of winter, I wonder about the broomsedge. Able to grow on nothing, holding the dirt, glowing like a sunset, perhaps it is the secret heart of winter.

Tasteless and uncompelling.

Unpalatable.

Every year in winter, I see the golden floes of broomsedge stretched out over different pastures and remember that this, this glorious golden abundance, is worthless.

A worthless plant.

About a hundred feet off the rushing pavement leans a wool grey barn, boards veined and curled with dryness and age. The pasture has relented to the frost and rain and huddles under a bare blanket of twisted hollow grass, brown and ashamed, hiding behind a protective hedge of gold weeds. The gentle beauty of a winter day drawn in charcoal and gold. It is a color, unremarkable in the riot of summer, but a feast during winter's famine.

Honey dripped over driftwood.

A breathtaking weed.

I can't decide whether to stop as long as I can stand the chill or
look away,
embarrassed by the splendor.
I know better than to pursue winter.
Winter is a time of rest.
Frozen and uninterpreted:
an unexplained landscape
of weeds and
longing.

Winter is full of uncomfortable things. Cold and wet and dangerous. The wind blows so hard across my front porch that our plastic furniture piles up on one end. We spend hours looking out the windows. It is winter; it is a dark, frozen time.

When wet mulch freezes the expanding ice crystals force the loose wood fibers up and out into odd jagged angles: a frozen earthquake. It looks like a tiny apocalyptic scene in a movie. It would be a movie where there's a giant earthquake and California finally becomes an island. Frozen mulch looks like the tiny mock-up you would make to visualize what the eruption of the entire San Andreas fault would look like. I am always temped to stomp the grotesque mulch ice-dancers down. I am intolerant of their non-conformity. I want to force these aberrations back into normalcy, embarrassed by their exposure.

They are too raw. Too vulnerable. Too grotesque. A tiny diorama of what our mountains must have looked like at their inception. Jagged and new but damp and fertile.

These misted, dripping mountains could not have been born of fire, they must have sprung from a cloud's love of the earth. The earth, damp and fresh, drawn skyward by her passion, reached for her heavenly lover who settled to his beloved low and cool, soothing and subtle. These mountains were born in a past so distant it has become secret.

Scandalous.
Shrouded.

They have become smoothed by their age, but they still long for the cloud, and the cloud still comes—wild and free: a lover born of wind and water. And in my garden the winter extrudes tiny frosty echoes of the past.

I once stood in front of an admissions officer at a small women's college and heard her say to me that because of the method of my schooling, my education was an "aberration." In the state of North Carolina, a child who is homeschooled must take a nationally standardized achievement test each year to ensure that he or she is receiving a thorough education, equivalent to his or her publically educated counterparts. Although I had been tested according to the laws of my state, and hers, and my test scores reported that I was a student worth consideration, she told me she could not reasonably evaluate me objectively and would be unable to consider any application that I would submit to her school. I was fourteen, long blond hair carefully pulled half back, and I was unpalatable—too grotesque to be considered.

As an adult, I am amused by her lack of both imagination and courage, but in ninth grade, all I could hear was that I was aberrant. I was an error. One that could not be accepted. I would not be considered as a potential student because I could not be evaluated by the usual or accepted means. But aberrant simply means outside the boundaries of normal, not valueless.

Twenty years later, I am standing again staring blankly into a situation I do not understand. Faces and lives stream past me, too fast to register while I am blank and useless. Chatter, events, and holidays flit past like squirrels. Everyone seems to have so much energy. People are doing things like redecorating their homes for holidays or taking family portraits or gardening, and I am standing here with all the pieces of normal life lying around me, abstract and undefined. Objects from some distant past. I just don't have the energy to push all the little pieces back into place. I keep picking them up and putting them back down. I no longer feel the desperate fire of grief and anger, I just feel stopped. I am not even sad or angry, I am just still. Like a waterfall frozen mid-drip. And all the bustle and life around me is as alien as I am. I feel so very wrong; so aberrant. I have been forced to step outside normal into a quiet place. I probably won't stay here. I am sure things are piling up while I am still, but just for now, I stand, exposed and awkward.

These metaphors are fanciful word pictures. Broomsedge is a pernicious weed. There is no mystery in a twisted spray of bark shreds. Water expands when it freezes. There is no passionate love affair between sky and earth. It's just misty here because of the humidity level. Winter is just winter and we must survive it. Winter comes to us all. We all long for the safety and ease of summer because, while winter is not valueless, it is hard. Water is turned to beautiful, cruel ice. The wind bites through layered up clothes and burns fingers and noses. The unsheltered die.

And still the trees tell us their story. Rings of rapid growth and slow growth wrapping around their core, paused by dormancy. A call for silence. Before the birds and bulbs and growth return. A stillness. Nature pauses. Does it listen? Perhaps. Perhaps not. But I watch them and learn. Life cannot always be about growth and change. My arboreal teachers have a century of wisdom. Simply allowing my heart and mind to freeze over and become grotesque and aberrant and silent right now is the bravest and only thing I can do.

CHAPTER 19

Footsteps

I AM NOT THE first to lose faith when things hurt. It is so cliché that I am almost embarrassed.

Almost.

When Moses, a man watching sheep in the desert, was confronted with the presence of God, he asked God who God was and God said, "I AM." I feel like Moses was probably less than satisfied with that answer. I AM leaves too much shrouded in mystery. I need to define and explain and assure myself that I have explained the mystery of God so that I know that I can rely on God to act the way that I want God to. God as a cosmic vending machine. If I pray correctly and discipline myself in a certain way, I can manipulate the cosmos into granting my three wishes. As long as I never do that and always tithe, I will find blessing upon blessing. And the needy and broken and sick? I will pray for them. And this djinn-God becomes the fountain of youth; a road to immortality.

If you are a good girl, Santa will bring you what you ask for.

I am the way, the truth and the life. No one comes to the Father except through me.

If you believe this, you will live forever.

And then when it all blows over, those without Koolaid mustaches shake their collective heads and sigh. How could they have fallen for that? It was just a story to keep them from being afraid of the dark. It was all just a story.

Religion may be an opiate for the masses, but God isn't. God is too wild and indefinable. God is what you know and demands more.

The whirl of a distant star, born a half zillion years ago, doesn't gleam with the fire of doctrine or theology, it burns with hydrogen and helium. I know that, but my secret, wild heart is thrilled by the notion that a star carries the spark of a creator. The God who is.

I AM.

The other day during school, my kids asked where God was and why we can't see God, and I sat there with my mind full of doubt and pain and disappointment and struggled to find words that were satisfying, concrete, and honest. I knew the easy answer. I knew what I felt. I knew the cliché.

God is everywhere. Unsatisfying.

God is. Abstract.

God is in heaven. Dishonest.

I couldn't say those things. So, I said this, "God is so big, that we cannot see God because we cannot imagine something big enough. It is like the whole universe is inside God's belly button and we look out and don't see a face, and figure we can't see God, but God is all around us." You can quote me on that.

We are God's belly button lint.

Then they asked where heaven is. And as a bereaved parent of bereaved children, I panicked. I don't know where heaven is. I don't even know what it is. I am not sure I even really believed in a real, tangible heaven until I heard my daughter whisper into my soul presumably from heaven. So, I said this: "I don't know where heaven is. But I know that there is one because your sister is there, and I can feel her there."

I do know heaven is not *up*. My best guess is that it is all around us like a world that is somehow more dimensioned than ours. Apparently, my understanding of heaven is closely related to a good sweater. All around me.

And hell? They didn't ask about it, but it seems a logical follow up. Sometimes I feel like there is more hell than heaven here. There are so many people who live every day in the grips of such pain that I know that I can't just wrap it up with pretty words and be done. I know a man who drifted into our town a few weeks before Gwyneth died. He is spectacularly bipolar. One day he is glowing with charm and as expansive as the horizon, and the next he has withdrawn within his hood, a soul in shadow. He came to Gwyneth's funeral. I remember that. He wore a Russian fur hat— respectfully. This man threatens to kill himself weekly. Surely, he lives with pain. Surely, that is enough hell for anyone? I don't know, but I imagine if there is a hell, it is a place of mirrors where you must confront yourself. And I also imagine, when you have learned to look and accept what you see and ask for forgiveness, your soul is welcomed to freedom and wholeness.

There is so much I don't know. Most days all I can do is scrape together just enough courage to believe there are things to ask questions about. I sit in my chair every morning (when the stars align and everyone sleeps through the night) and stare out the window at the sunrise. Sometimes I look pleadingly, sometimes belligerently, and sometimes, just every so often, with expectation. I don't know what I am looking for. At one point in my life, I would have called it prayer, but I am not praying. It can't be called meditation either because it isn't that organized. I am just looking. My spiritual practice has been reduced to the equivalent of a newborn's blank, uncomprehending, undemanding stare.

In the fourteenth chapter of the Gospel of John, Jesus tells one of his disciples that he, Jesus, is our way to the Father. A pathway to the incomprehensible. The problem is, these words, given to a terrified man, Thomas, have been taken up and used to bludgeon the world. You (thud) must (thud) believe (thud) in (thud) Jesus (thud). It hurts.

I am the way, the truth and the life. No one comes to the Father except through me.

When Jesus left the church a couple thousand years ago, his followers knew there was something profound about the life and witness of this man. They had seen him, touched his hands, seen his tears and cleansed his torn body. They knew life was now different. Christianity wasn't a religion. It wasn't even a moral code. Those baptized into the first church just were. They were millers and potters and fishers and tent makers who had seen God.

Jesus gives us a way to blindly grope our way towards a God we were never intended to grasp. I do believe in God, but I do not understand God. But this man, Jesus. Jesus is the Word. Jesus is God. Jesus is man. And I can look at Jesus and find my way forward just one step. I will never find a way to understand Noah and the bones in the water, but I do know that a man who welcomed children and grieved with real salty tears, is a man who gives me hope.

A woman is pregnant for about thirty-eight weeks. During that time two zygotes are fused together into the single cell: a one walled world containing the helix that will shape a life. The height and breadth of the person is hidden away in the inner sanctuary of this completed cell and slowly revealed as the cell divides and differentiates into the child we will name. What starts as two halves of a whole must become, exponentially, the harbor for a soul.

For twenty-nine weeks, a new life, separate from my own has struggled to multiply and grow within the walls of my body—a heartbeat that doesn't match my own. My body has done this five times. It is tired. Each day, I struggle to protect and nourish and carry this child becoming more and more exhausted by the effort of moving. My body is shoved aside into pockets of aches and unfortunate shapes. My blood vessels throb and bulge under the weight of new growth.

Before they took their first breath, I knew my children. I knew my first was dreamy. I knew my second was vibrant and fierce. I knew my third was silly and strong. I knew my fourth was sweet and gentle. And I still know that. I knew when her ashes blew onto the ancient mountainside that she was my sunny sweet child. Still with me. A saint. But I am overwhelmed by the pain of separation. Because if she still is with me, and she is, then: God. And damn it, if God, then why is she not with me? If God, then how do I turn my blinded eyes and tear-streaked face from the edge of the waters of death and live?

I am the way, the truth, and the life.

Jesus. Jesus made footprints in the dirt. His fingernails bent back when he caught them on the edge of his shirt. He ate real food and preferred his fish cooked over charcoal. He enjoyed a loving touch. He was and is and he can lead us to his Father. I will be safe if I place my feet in his footprints like a child following her father through the snow. Perhaps, these words, so often quoted to exclude, were meant to assure. Change the voice, change the tone. "Don't worry, I am the way. All you have to do is follow me. Don't worry, I have shown you truth. Believe in the simple way of love. Don't worry, I am alive, and so are you. Come now, tender soul, and I will take you to my Father, heaven knows, you won't get there alone." And sitting here, my soul settles. Yes. Yes, this is a small truth, a small shiver of grace.

Is God? There is no evidence. No fossils or shrouds or climbable mountains. It is easier to say no. No, life is a chaotic system. No one is missing your pain. No one is ambivalent to the murder of men, kidnapped and hero-less, whose blood is washed away by the same water that covered the bones of all mankind. I am safe in the anonymity of chaos, broken but unforgotten.

I am annoyed by my dissatisfaction with atheism. Am I a coward? Am I a romantic? Do I have the courage to admit that there might be a being, an "I am?"

And this fifth baby? Do I have the courage to know her? To love her? Knowing that, if she lives or dies, my heart will break? It is this final thing that gives me the strength to step onto the dusty road behind the man Jesus. Is it crazy to believe in God? Probably. Yes, it probably is, but I can't not. I tried. I wanted to. But there is a wild song that I can hear between the beats of my heart that will not stop. I will never understand the bones beneath the water or the ashes on the wind, but I will follow the one who loved the children as I do because it is my only way.

This baby is wild and tough, and I love her—courageous or not.

CHAPTER 20

Prayer, Part 2

I WAS WRONG.

I can still pray.

I am sitting at my computer looking out a new window. The old window served its purpose; it gave me a focus for my sadness and my grief, and I am grateful to it. But this new window faces east, and, from where I sit, I can see the sunrise. Trees, black against the white sky, frame my view, mist clinging to their branches like sleep. The trees are in leaf, and, here, too, there is a branch exposed by trauma. It appears, if ashamed, brave. There is a generous streaking of clouds, not clouds hinting at a day of rain but more of the painter's-focal-point type of cloud. They are cream and gold and purple and they seem to hang on the horizon, trapped by my eye. The sky has gone from the white of early sunrise to blue, so I know that this day has decided to begin too.

Prayer is a scary idea. It is the idea that a created soul can communicate with its creator with vested interest. Or maybe that's not quite right.

The sky has tightened into a yellow-gold shout. It has become sky! The dew on the leaves and the mist are shining and the trees, magnificently backlit, have gone black by contrast. The clouds have all shifted. I didn't see them move even though I was watching. My breath wants to stop when I look, like the moment must be a breath-holding moment, but it is too long and too bright. I can't keep my eyes trained on it. It is too glorious and mundane.

Prayer had become something that didn't or couldn't or wouldn't.

We prayed for her every day,
> *but the cancer in her breasts still killed her.*

We prayed for him,
> *but he didn't change.*

We prayed for reconciliation,
> *but we ended up hurt.*

Could it be that I didn't ask in faith? If we had asked, would Gwyneth, like Jarus's daughter, have woken to us?

The sky has begun to press toward me with a shimmer bordering on prismatic. The whole sky has gone white hot like molten metal. It seems like a miracle. All the clouds are gone and the trees are rising from black to green. I am squinting a bit. I feel like I can't look away or I will miss it, but I have been watching this show for an hour and a half. Although I know it won't come, I am hoping for some spectacular finale. Perhaps this time, the sun and clouds and mist and trees will join hands and bow while the birds sing a reprise, and I will be released, having completed my task of observing the sunrise. But instead, of course, day and its demands and tasks take over, and the sunrise is over? Complete? I don't know, perhaps a sunrise ends at noon when the sun begins to tend toward setting?

I can pray now. But I have discovered that prayer is different. I do not ask. I can't ask because what I want isn't possible. So, I don't ask, I just fill my head with space, like blowing a bubble in a good piece of gum, and let the God of sunrise well up inside it. I know that God sees my pain and the pain of the world. I know that God does not require my insistence to act on behalf of God's children, but there is some need for me to become a larger vessel. There is some reason for me to create more space in my self for God. Perhaps it is so my soul can, like the sun, rise.

The sky! is too bright to look at. The light is stretched across the carpet. The sun is up, balanced on the tiniest tips of the trees. The sky seems to pulse with poetry or music, begging me to, please, record its beauty, but my kids are awake and the day must begin. I won't see the end of this show because breakfast is more immediate than the sublime, but I will steal five more minutes. Five more minutes before shoes and socks and cereal.

How can one mother, hidden away behind laundry and three meals a day, remain visible? How can pain and grief become elegant? I don't know. I don't know, but the aim and purpose that I see, that I can feel trembling at the edges of my vision, will be achieved like the sunrise. So I will add one more confusing simile to Jesus's: The Kindgom of God is like a sunrise. Insistent, glorious, silent, mundane, slow, illuminating, and best of all, one hundred percent free to all.

Today I returned to the river. The water is low because we haven't had enough rain. Rocks lay exposed on the bank, prime for throwing. The national park is full of people, but this little stretch of the river is deserted. It feels as if these rocks have lain here, growing moss and waiting for us, since the earth first whirled into existence. The trees line the banks of the river conjuring mist in their leaves and wrapping us in a harbor of safety. I snap pictures while three tiny, wiry daredevils dip farther and farther into the sixty-degree water. Whoops and shouts echo down the riverbed as the triumphant rise, dripping and reddened with the cold. On the rock next to me a tiny forest of moss and miniature plants is growing. Behind me is the forest floor thick with leaf rot and black, loamy earth. I wonder at the plants on the rock. Don't they know? Life would be so much easier over there.

We have grown. The five-year-old has stretched into a seven-year-old and is heaving his own huge rocks into the deepest pools. The new five-year-old has stripped down to her leggings and her hair is shaggy around her face making her look like a daughter of this place—Mowgali's blonde sister drenched in the water of a cold mountain river. There is a three-year-old whose ribs stand out in protest against the drip and grit of the play. He howls in effort as he raises a soggy log over his head and heaves it into the water. I have a new baby in my arms now. Her head is fuzzy and her drool ropes down my arm and drips into the water. Her thighs are a chubby ode to breastfeeding. She gets splashed and her face goes all twisted up and shocked. I pile them up on the bank and take their picture. One dad and four kids. Our grins are manic and wide and gap-toothed. We are here, together, wet and wild. On the way home we will stop at Gwyneth's place and leave flowers. We will take a picture there too.

I don't know if I will ever fully forgive God for Gwyneth's death.

Perhaps the death of a child is too big a thing to forgive.

Perhaps the anger and hurt never fade,

Perhaps I don't want to feel better.

Sometimes it feels like betrayal to heal, but at this moment, for this day, I can say that I feel like a person in a wingsuit who has just stepped into thin air. Do I know that this suit will fly? Do I know my arms are strong enough to hold this air until I land safely?

No. I don't know, but it is worth the thrill of flight to try.

The tears in my eyes are equal parts grief and joy and hope. I won't wait to make it sometime in the future, I am making it now. Sometimes my heart is broken and sometimes I laugh without noticing. I will not wait to heal completely to live, but I will not live broken forever. Time is healing even this. Even me. It feels like a betrayal to let the pain go. I certainly haven't forgotten, but you can only swim against the river of time for so long. Sometimes, oddly, I miss the days of immediate sorrow. She seemed so close then. I still feel her with me, but it is just like any child growing up, they become more distinctly them and less you. Even though my children are quite literally flesh of my flesh and bone of my bone, they are not me, and by the time they are three they are running and jumping and throwing rocks, and even if you wanted to keep them with you always, they are built to fly.

And so am I.
And so I will.